Wealth Creation & Financial Statement Analysis

Dream to be Wealthy

"Can You Smell Money"

"If you don't find a way to make money while you sleep, you will work until you die.-

Warren Buffett

Vivek Choudhary

To

My Hero Warren Buffett

PREFACE

"It is better to conquer yourself than to win a thousand battles. Then the victory is yours. It cannot be taken from you."

-Buddha 400 BCE

Dream to be wealthy is a book for all the people who wish to be wealthy, wealth cannot be created in a day or a month, it takes time but definitely wealth will be created. Since our childhood, our parents always advised us to save money. Today's banks are ready to lend you money with interest; so that you can fulfil your desire but it is more important than first we should have enough earning so that can fulfil our basic needs. I have shared you the guideline principles, how you can use this principle to create wealth for ourselves and to enjoy financial freedom. Creating wealthy is based on your behaviour and your own integrity, discipline & dedication and your will power to be dedicated not to lose your sight. This book will guide us how we move forward in your lives and not to be trap in the rat race, you should able to understand how to make money and again I am saying making money is not so easy it is a completely

Up to you how you behave as Warren Buffett said *"if you don't find a way to make money while you sleep you will work until you die"*.

You should have enough wealth for your good life; you need to ask yourself, why we are here? What is the purpose to be here in this world? And to know your purpose and how to fulfil your a dream? The process I am sharing in this book is a road map navigator to find the hidden treasure to become wealthy and if you use it wisely in your daily life, you will be going to be very wealthy, I don't have any doubts about it, and we all need financial freedom and a great peace of mind. When I was young my parents used to advise that I should save money for a good future. The first law to become wealthy is to start saving and invest your money in different kind of investment from there you will get a good return, you can use the eighth wonder of the world that is compound interest, Albert Einstein famously said that compound interest is the most powerful force in the universe. He said, "Compound interest is the 8th wonder of the world. He, who understands it, earns it; he who doesn't, pays it." Once you will be wealthy, you will be financially free; you can generate a good wealth for yourself and your family. Before we start this book it is very important first to trust ourselves and to ask ourselves, why can't I be wealthy? When in this world so much wealth is available and people are becoming wealthy and that is not strange.

"Someone will always be getting richer faster than you. This is not a tragedy."

— Charlie Munger

When wealth is available, why it is not coming to me, we will discuss how great investors like Warren Buffett uses investing principal to create wealth.

Introduction

"If you buy things you do not need, soon you will have to sell things you need."

— Warren Buffett

"You don't have to be brilliant, only a little bit wiser than the other guys, on average, for a long time."

--Charlie Munger

This book is the understanding and observing how some of the wealthy people on planet have created wealth in their life and we can learn from their habit. We can use same process principle to create wealth for ourselves. I have divided the book in eight sections, each section we will learn how to create wealth. Charlie Munger famously said **"Live within your income and save so that you can invest. Learn what you need to learn."**

The first section in this book it about the creation of wealth, the importance of wealth, the habit we can learn from some of the wealthy people and develop the same skill, why rich people try to look wealthy but broke in couple years, where they made the mistake, we will see what was wrong with rich people that they cannot become wealthy, going forward we understand what kind of rules are there to become wealthy and how to get wealthy.

In this book, we will go through how leverage destroys people and make them broke, well said by warren Buffett in interview on CNBC "It is crazy in my view to borrow money on securities. It's insane to risk what you have and need for something you don't really need… You will not be way happier if you double your net worth." he also mentioned "My partner Charlie (Munger) says there are only three ways a smart person can go broke: liquor, ladies, and leverage. Now the truth is — the first two he just added because they started with L — it's leverage."

We will go through the details to become financially free. Saving and investment is very important and how much we should save and what type of income, we can create to become financially free, we will see an example of people who created enormous wealth through passive income thought using stock investing and they are wealthy people in this world .We will understand the value of money, for present value as well as future value.

we see also learn the history of stock investing, how to invest, how to go through selecting a good and quality company for that I have shared the Apple Inc financial statement like balance sheet, income statement and cash flow and some important ratio analysis, we will also learn the valuable lesson from great investors like Warren Buffett, Peter Lynch, Charlie Munger, and Benjamin Graham.

What you will learn:-

- How to create wealth?
- Why some people is wealthy and that is not a tragedy?
- What wealthy people know, that we don't know?
- What habit should I perceive to become wealthy?
- What I will do today for my better tomorrow?
- What is financial freedom?
- To be financially free, what kind of income I require?

- How to invest in a stock?
- How to select a quality company for investing?
- What is the power of investing?
- How greatest investor created wealth?
- How to quit the rat race in order to live a wealthy life and enjoy the financial freedom?

About the Author

Vivek Choudhary is a Value Investor & Entrepreneur who has over 20 years of experience in investment and entrepreneurship. Involve in diversify business Commodities, Manufacturing, Hotel & Automobiles.

He earned MBA in finance & Marketing at IIPM, MDP in Strategic Market Planning at IIM, Equity Research Analyst at BSE Institute, Value Investing at Stanford University Continue studies, and Entrepreneurship Essential & Leading with Finance at HBX Harvard Business School & Value Investing at Columbia Business School, Business Lesson Cohort at Harvard Business School Online.

He is passionate about Value Investing and invests globally. His hobby is reading. Every day he read value investing books and finance books.

He admires his Hero Mr. Warren Buffett Chief Executive Officer of Berkshire Hathaway – He follows his footprint Value Investing. For him, reading and studying are like compounding it will help him in achieving his passion.

He wrote the book:-

- **Value Investing & Behavioral Finance**

- **Wealth Creation & Financial Statement Analysis "Dream to be Wealthy"**

- **Value Investing - Legendary Graham & Dodd Valuation**

- **Value Investing CHECKLIST**

- **Billionaires Mind – Blue Print of Entrepreneurship**

- **Why Investors Fail –Mistakes Value Investors Avoid**

www.security-analysis.com

CONTENTS

Preface   III

Introduction   VI

Introduction to Wealth

1. Wealth — 2
2. Importance of Wealth — 7
3. Habit to be Wealthy — 13
4. Rich Vs Wealthy — 21
5. Rules to be Wealthy — 32
6. How to Get Wealthy — 39
7. Leverage — 48
8. Financial Freedom — 51
9. Power of Investing — 58
10. Income Type — 76
11. Power of Stock Investing — 94
12. Time Value of Money — 110

CONTENTS

Stock Investing & Company Analysis

| 13 | Stock Investing | 119 |
| 14 | Financial Statement | 131 |

Income Statement

15	Income Statement	138
16	Revenue	141
17	Cost of Goods Sold	144
18	Gross Profit	147
19	Operating expenses	150
20	S ,G & A	152
21	R & D	155
22	Operating Income	158
23	Other Income /Expenses ,Net	160
24	EBIT	162
25	Provision for Income Tax	164
26	Net income	166
27	Earnings Per Share	168

CONTENTS

Balance Sheet

28	Balance Sheet	171
29	Cash & Cash Equivalents	176
30	Marketable Securities	179
31	Accounts Receivable, Net	182
32	Inventories	185
33	Vendor Non –Trade Receivable	187
34	Other Currents Assets	189
35	Total currents Assets	191
36	Marketable Securities	193
37	PPE ,Net	195
38	Other Non –Current Assets	198
39	Total Non –Current Assets	200
40	Total Assets	201
41	Accounts Payable	203
42	Other Current Liabilities	205
43	Deferred Revenue	207
44	Commercial Paper	209
45	Terms Debts	212
46	Total Current Liabilities	214
47	Long –Term Debts	216
48	Other Non –Current Liabilities	219
49	Total Non –Current Liabilities	221

CONTENTS

50 Total Shareholders' Equity — 222

Cash Flow Statement

51 Cash Flow Statement — 226
52 Operating Activities — 230
53 Investing Activities — 232
54 Financing activities — 234
55 Free Cash Flow — 236

Valuation of Stock

56 Discounted Cash Flow — 239

Ratio Analysis

57 Ratio Analysis — 248
- Current ratio — 248
- Inventory Turnover Ratio — 249
- Assets Turnover Ratio — 250
- Gross Profit Margin — 250
- Operating Profit Margin — 251
- Net Profit Margin — 252
- Return on Assets — 253
- Debts to Equity Ratio — 254

CONTENTS

Great Investor Strategy

58 Great Investor Strategy   256

- Benjamin Graham   259
- Warren Buffett   265
- Peter Lynch   270
- Charlie Munger   278

Introduction to Wealth

"Formal education will make you a living; self-education will make you a fortune."

—Jim Rohn

1
Wealth

"Life is like a snowball. The important thing is finding wet snow and a really long hill."

— Warren Buffett

Wealth is financial freedom, to know about wealth first we should know about the history of money. Significant evidence state that earlier in the Asian Barter system happened in the market that could be described as a medium exchange this includes livestock and grains that people use to exchange with communities, this kind of exchange is described as barter. The history of bartering dates all the way back to 6000 BC. Introduced by Mesopotamia tribes, bartering was adopted by the Phoenicians. Phoenicians bartered goods to those located in various other cities across oceans. Babylonians also developed an improved bartering system. Bartering is a very old concept. It was the sole form of purchasing goods and services between individuals earlier than the creation of currency. In spite of the fact that economics has significantly developed, bartering is just as legitimate today. Human life and activities are very simple in the initial stages. When people start their journey, at that time there was not any money.

People traded items with items (i.e. corn may be exchanged for cloth, house for horses, bananas for oranges, and so on), and sometimes precious goods were used as a measurement of exchange. Barter system works well in such a traditional society where economic production is less, economic development is low and exchange is little.

Today money has taken a different form like we have gold, we have currency, even now we are using a cashless system like we are using internet banking and using a credit card, even today gold stand belonging to history but even today many rich people were in a different part of the world keep some of their wealth in the form of gold. Today Currency is the face value which is used as a medium of exchange. Money allows people to trade goods and services. Wealth is a concept which was originated in the year 1990 in the United States, it is financial planning. People like Warren Buffett, the most successful investor in the world has created billions of dollars and his basic approach is to allocate capital, diversified business in such a way that all the return should be above the cost of capital. What he always says that a stock is not something that triggers a symbol that reflects in the market it is a business behind the stock and we should know all about the companies.

We should understand what kind of investments we can do and how we can use the Asset allocation so that we can make enough wealth, as we have a dream in our life. We need to do proper financial planning to get a successful return. Today's world people face losses in their financial issues due to not having proper knowledge about financial planning, how to beat the inflation and able to generate more return on capital. Equity investing has proven that it has given a good return in a long horizon and surpass all other investment, we should be having a proper goal for the kind of return we are looking from our investing, We can create wealth to meet our different responsibility in our life, like when we are unmarried we have a different responsibility and when we are married we have different responsibility and when will be old then we will have different, to meet our life goal, we should be knowing what kind of return we are looking in stock investing. Stock investing over time creates enough wealth as compared with a mutual fund. The mutual fund has lots of share in their portfolio and the return will be not much as the individual who is doing our own research and investing, you can easily able to perform better than the mutual fund as you will be selecting only selected stock that will be going to perform in long run and you are not going to for the sake of diversification.

There are different sets of asset classes where you can invest like in mutual fund, real estate but if you compare with this stock market give more return compare with all the other investment options.

Most of our life, we will be earning and spending our money, if we will earn more money then only we can only fulfil our desire. To fulfil our desire we borrow money, only when our current income exceeds our expenditure.

Why do we need to save? how it will change my life, if you invest $100 and after one year you receive $120, so you will get 20% of the return for the investment for one year, this is a way to create wealth.

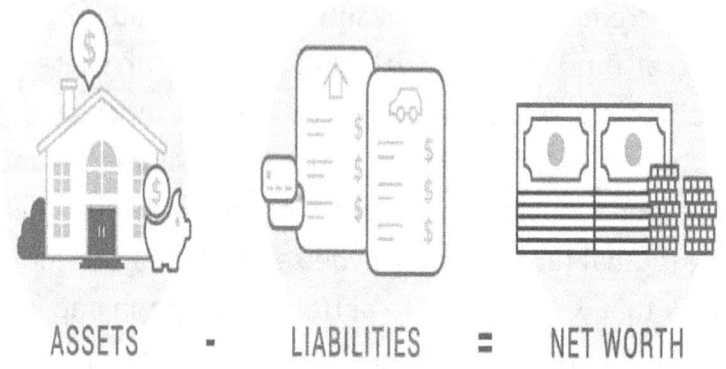

ASSETS - LIABILITIES = NET WORTH

2
Importance of Wealth

Rich people believe "You can have your cake and eat it too." Middle-class people believe "Cake is too rich, so I'll only have a little piece." Poor people don't believe they deserve cake, so they order a doughnut, focus on the hole, and wonder why they have "nothing."

— T. Harv Eker —

Wealth: the individual current value of all Asset minus liability, if the assets exceed we call it a net worth. Warren Buffett is an American Businessman investor who is the current chairman and CEO of Berkshire Hathaway he has considered one of the most successful investors in the world is net worth is $88.9 billion dollars. Value can be intangible and tangible that makes a person or a family to be wealthy, where accounting value is tangible cash land building or intangible is patent copyright and trademark that have a potential to generate future income that can create a person to be wealth. One of the secret behind the success is, if you would have invested in Berkshire Hathaway $800 in 1962 it would be now $300000 in 2019 simple formula is to hold the stock of a company. When we invest in a good company then we'll see how it generates a good return and you can see the example of Warren Buffett.

Warren Buffett said you don't need to be a rocket scientist investor "investing is not a game where the guy with 160 IQ beat the guy with a 130 IQ "what in need is emotional stability, you need to think independently, it doesn't matter where are you right now but what you can become is more important, what you have and what you can do now is important to create wealth.

The importance of being wealthy depends on us. If you can create wealth then you can maintain your standard on living, to retire healthy, and to live your life as you want and you can able to follow your passion, people say that money isn't everything but I would say before making such statement you should have created enough wealth. Money provides you the freedom and controls your life and not to evolve in the rat race, refer to a competitive struggle to get ahead financially. In this modern world, many are living in rats in a single maze, expend a lot of effort running around, and ultimately achieving nothing.

This is often used in reference to work, particularly excessive or competitive work; in general, terms, if one works too much, one is "in the rat race". A key aspect of the rat race is being inflicted on the individual by uncontrollable outside forces such as researchers in the case of literal rats in a laboratory maze, or the inherent logic, pressures, and incentives of contemporary businesses and society (e.g. productivity, acceleration, and status). This terminology contains implications that many people see work as a seemingly endless pursuit with little reward or purpose. *"Most people never get wealthy simply because they are not trained financially to recognize opportunities right in front of them. The rich have learned to recognize opportunities as well as how to create them"*

-Robert Kiyosaki

Income is routinely mistaken for wealth. For example, if Dennis's income is $50,000 per year, some people might say Dennis is "wealthy." However, if Dennis has to pay the mortgage, car payments, student loans from medical school, medical bills for his child, and private school tuition for his other child consume most of his monthly income, he may not have much left for saving at the end of the month. Consequently, Dennis may have a nice house, but he has virtually nothing saved up for retirement or emergencies. That is, he may have a high income, but he is not "wealthy" because he owns little of the things in his life.

Wealth doesn't mean in living a luxurious life i.e. for buying expensive cars, living in the expensive house but it more into the financial freedom, that when you wake up to live your passion, it is nothing to do with the house you living, an example of Warren Buffett is living in the same house, the house he bought in 1958. His passion is to create wealth to enjoy his financial freedom to control of his life, most people think that to be wealthy is to have a lot of money luxurious shiny objects, sports car and many more and that is the often associated with success but the real success is not this to be successful, you should behave enough assets than a liability.

Wealth can be generated through passive income, the investment of $10,000 and income generated $100000 from that without working which is the magic and power of stock investing. Your wealth should be enough to cover monthly expenses then only we can be wealthy, one can choose to stop working and still living and maintaining his lifestyle. Lots of movie star and sports star earn millions of dollar but they went bankrupt in couple of years because you don't understand the power of saving and their lifestyle is beyond the income ability and doesn't allow them to save. The one who makes the most money may not be wealthy

Money is by-product and is always be by-product take a look at the most of the highly wealthy people like Warren Buffet, Bill Gates they live a simple Lifestyle rather than spending all the billions of dollars in maintaining social status, they use the money for a bigger and better cause, highly successful people believe that money is a vehicle of hard work, they do not focus on making the most money, they focus on building the business and chasing their passion.

In today's world, people are becoming more materialistic than ever, they want to compare with others when they see people post a picture of a new car in Facebook or somebody is going for holiday, so they also wish for the same, might be they need to borrow money to fulfil desire . Money is important without money is no way you can buy food or survive. Money can help you achieving your goal but unfortunately the media and our society has made us believe that money is everything buying a luxurious car is not about your wealth , what if living in the same house but still not wealthy it is not about how much you have spend rather than how much you have saved.

Money can buy your freedom give your more choice in your life, spend on the more important things in such as being with your family and the people that you love, you can choose as per your wish to spend your time and to continue to work or to retire.

you can enjoy lots of freedom in your life when you are wealthy and that the importance of being wealthy, you can make your dream possible related to the money and finally it will allow you to contribute to the society and make the world a better place as you can donate a portion of your money to help and support greater cause just like Bill Gates and Warren Buffett pledge to donate and help to make the world a better place.

3

Habit to Be Wealthy

> Most people never get wealthy simply because they are not trained financially to recognize opportunities right in front of them. The rich have learned to recognize opportunities as well as how to create them
>
> — *Robert Kiyosaki* —

Wealthy speak the language of money. Wealthy people are more financially literate than the poor. They're better educated about personal finance. Because they know what they're talking about, they're better able to advocate for themselves. They're able to make better decisions.

They understand that money is a long game. Or, put another way, wealthy people recognize that there's no reliable way to get rich quickly but that almost anyone can get rich slowly. The keys are persistence and patience. Do the right things for a long time and you will achieve your financial goals? "The choice is not between this $5 Starbucks that will make me happy or this $5 investing. "The choice is between this $5 Starbucks today or the hundreds of dollars it has the potential to be when it comes time for retirement."

Wealthy peoples save 40% of the net income and live on the remaining 60%. Financial knowledge is important to create wealth, wealthy people read every day, and to become a wealthy person they need to have knowledge about basic finance so that you can understand how financial world work. Wealthy People watch less TV and spend less time in using the internet, this is a kind of habit they develop, wealthy people love their job, whatever they do, they are very passionate of doing that job because they know that success comes when you are passionate about your work, that means if you are investing you should be very focused on investing should be known in and out what is happening, you should have a very clear vision.

Wealthy people don't give up so easily they work really hard to chase their dream by doing so they are among the few people who can able to create wealth for themselves and they believe in themselves, saving is one of the very important aspects of becoming wealthy. It doesn't matter is which situation currently you are living but if you want to be wealthy then you have to change your mentality the way you think, you should set a higher goal and you should have proper planning to achieve that goal and when it comes stock investing you see all the billionaires in this world have only two investing ways one is by doing business and second is buying stock in a business.

Wealthy people success is not defined as an intelligent, talented or charm but instant the difference are in there daily habits that differentiate rich, wealthy and poor, like wealthy people with an annual gross income of $ 150000 and the net liquid asset is $3.2 million but as those with the gross income of $25,000 or less and no more than $ 5000 in liquidation.

The habit to be formed to live within your means like limit your entertainment spend, less to auto loans, stay away from the credit card and think you should save and then to invest the money to make the money compound for you building a successful life. Wealthy people have a very good reading habit, autobiography of successful people, self-development books, and wealthy didn't wish just to achieve their goal but they have proper planning a goal orientation.

Their investment is to gain knowledge, these people often don't buy a very sporty car or think that it is worthless and if buy only when required.

77 percent of those who struggle financially play the lottery. Hardly anyone who is wealthy plays the numbers. Wealthy people do not rely on random good luck for their wealth. They create their own good luck. If you still want to bet after knowing the risk, use money from your entertainment budget.

Not every emotion needs to be expressed. When you say whatever is on your mind, you risk hurting others. Loose lips are a habit for 69 percent of those who struggle financially. Conversely, 94 percent of wealthy people filter their emotions. They understand that letting emotions control is important if not can destroy relationships at work and at home. Wait to say what's on your mind until you're calm and have had time to look at the situation objectively, make them invaluable to their employers or customers, writing articles related to their industry, speaking at industry events and networking. Successful people work hard to achieve the mutual goals of their employers or their businesses. You cannot control the outcome of a wish, but you can control the outcome of a goal.

Every year, 70 percent of the wealthy pursue at least one major goal. Only 3 percent of those struggling to make ends meet do this. Wealthy people are good communicators because they are good listeners. They understand that you can learn and educate yourself only by listening to what other people have to say. We are only as successful as the people we spend the most time with, of wealthy, successful people, 86 percent associate with other successful people. But 96 percent of those struggling financially stick with others struggling financially. Among the wealthy, 93 percent who had a mentor attributed their success to that person. Mentors regularly and actively participate in your growth by teaching you what to do and what not to do. Finding such a teacher is one of the best and least painful ways to become rich.

If you know your goals, find someone who has already achieved them. You'll be amazed by how many people want to lend a helping hand. Those struggling financially in life have a way of creating bad luck for themselves. It's a by-product of their habits. Poverty Habits, repeated over and over are like snowflakes on a mountainside. In time, these snowflakes build up until the inevitable avalanche—a preventable medical problem, a lost job, a failed marriage, a broken business relationship, or a bankruptcy.

Conversely, successful people create their own unique type of good luck. Their positive habits lead to opportunities such as promotions, bonuses, new business, and good health. Coupled with healthy eating, wealthy people also believe in staying fit by exercising. Millionaires may be busy people, but they nearly always find time in their days to work out. In fact, Corley reports that 76% of wealthy folks do aerobic exercise at least four days per week, compared to 23% of poor people. Setting goals is crucial to achieving wealth, but if it were the only requirement then nearly everyone would be rich. For the wealthy, setting specific goals and writing them down is a winning habit that works.

There's a popular saying that you have to spend money to make money. While this is true, most non-wealthy people don't take into account the fact that the more money you spend, the less you have – and spending more than you earn does not result in wealth.

Wealthy people avoid overspending. Just because they could throw down half a million dollars for a brand new car doesn't mean they do. The wealthy invest their time in comparison shopping and negotiation, getting the best deals for their dollars and saving more money than they spend. They develop reasonable budgets with a service like Personal Capital and stick to them.

Wealthy people understand that risks lead to rewards, and as a result, they're more willing to go out on a limb – though they generally take calculated risks, not reckless ones. Furthermore, the rich know exactly what they stand to lose if a risk fails to deliver its reward. They are more likely to have contingency plans in place to minimize potential fallout in the event that things don't go according to plan.

Charity and philanthropy are hallmarks of the wealthy. Those who are wealthy and successful tend to be generous with their wealth. Examples throughout history support this – from Nelson Rockefeller and Andrew Carnegie to Carlos Slim and Bill Gates. Giving back to the community and improving the world is an important characteristic for the wealthy.

While the wealthy may have extensive savings and vast retirement portfolios, they generally have no intention of retiring or at least, not as early as others. According to a Gallup poll, the average retirement age for Americans is 61, but the majority of wealthy people don't plan to retire until at least 70 – not because they have to keep working, but because they want to.

The longer you continue to work, the more money you can make. The drive to stay healthy is connected to this goal. Wealthy people often choose not to retire, and since the majority enjoy what they do, the idea of continuing to work is both welcome and comforting.

4

Rich Vs Wealthy

"Being rich is having money; being wealthy is having time." - Margaret Bonnano

If we compare between the rich versus wealthy we found that out that all we have 24 hours in a day and we need to handle our working hours so well that we can create more money and believe that one day will be wealthy. If you see rich people earn their money in a number of ways may be win lottery on in few shots in year compare with wealthy make money by a business owner, there is a big difference between two bridge and somebody who is rich have lots of money to spend the fancy cars, the fancy and go to a fancy restaurant, what does it describe that he is a wealthy person or there is a difference between the wealthy and the rich person. The major difference between rich and wealthy is the question here needs to be asked how long the money will last. Once earning is going to pass on the next generation! The Wealthy person keeps wealth for the multiple generations, compare with rich people that why the money which has been earning on to lottery winning it's just going in a short.

Wealthy people know how to make money, you can make a renewable wealth like Warren Buffett investment as early you start saving and investing

Different between wealthy and rich as rich have lots of money but have habits of expenditure, were compared to wealthy people who don't have. Wealthy don't waste money in the things they don't need but rich people spend lots of money instead of investing for the money they buy expensive cars ,houses and expensive lifestyle, that doesn't matter what you make in a year if not going to save in single penny, is better to make 60000 dollar in a year save 50% off that invest by the time you will make lots of money very well the common example we can see that when you meet a wealthy person he will be very simple compared to the person who is rich due to its habit, as rich must be wearing expensive clothes, expensive watches but he is not wealthy, if you see there are celebrities well-known due to their habit has gone into bankruptcy compare with this billionaire Warren Buffett he still live in the same house that he purchased back in 1954 just over $30,000 and wealthy people need to do lots of sacrifices in his early age to gain wealth. Rich people think become superior they are very happy but at the end of the day when they have to make the EMI payment to the bank interest when they become bankrupt, the actually know where they are. Difference between rich and wealthy is that people who make lots of money but all the money goes into the lifestyle and every time they make a little on they go for shopping and even buy a bigger house and new sports car, which result in long-term debt and both hard about nothing is left, this kind of behavior that separates the rich.

People don't know the difference between rich and wealthy, it is important to live a financial freedom life compare to rich people have lots of collection of expensive paintings, collecting different types of antique compared to the wealthy person need security in life.

Rich want the social status in Prestige associate with the million-dollar club versus wealthy people never run out of the wealth they know the secret to preserving the wealth compare with rich people they know how to destroy the wealth.

Most people don't realize this, but the two have one extremely important difference. Understanding that difference is a huge key to reaching financial freedom

Rich people are motivated to live a high lifestyle but wealthy people are motivated by their passion and dream.

Rich people have won millions of dollars, spend it like crazy, and now it's all gone.

That lottery winner may have the money, but it was only for a short time. He wasn't able to preserve it for the next generation to enjoy that fortune but wealthy families possess the gift of knowledge; a deeper understanding of sustaining their wealth and preserving for the generations and years to come. Take a look at the billionaires of this generation. Bill Gates and Mark Zuckerberg.

Wealthy people keep it simple, wearing the same clothes and getting into cars that regular people use as they get richer and richer, they didn't excessively change their spending habits. They could lead a lavish lifestyle if they want to; after all, they can afford to be extravagant but no. These billionaires understand the value of making money, spending only on what's practical. They are wealthy individuals, not just rich, and are financial independence. There must be freedom from the thought of money troubles.

According to Mr. Kiyosaki, the state of being wealthy is determined by the number of days where you can survive and not worry about money that are coming in.

It pertains to the days where you don't have to work yet still maintain your standard of living. To be wealthy is not about what you can buy. It's about being able to sustain your lifestyle and your existence without the need to work.

Some examples of what wealthy people wear vs. ich People wear?

Wealthy People wear

Bill Gates and his $50 Casio Quartz Diver Watch

Warren Edward Buffett net worth $ 88 Billion, with Bill Gates net worth $98 billion.

Rich People wear

50 Cent managed to finish paying off more than $22 million (£16.9 million), and was discharged from bankruptcy.

Mike Tyson was $23 million (£18 million) in debt and filed for bankruptcy in 2003.

($1.3 billion) in debt accumulated by Kingfisher Airlines, which shut down in 2012

Eike Fuhrken Batista da Silva (Brazilian Portuguese; born 3 November 1956) is a Brazilian-German serial entrepreneur who made and lost a fortune in mining and oil and gas industries. He engaged in a quest to promote Brazil's infrastructure with large-scale projects, such as the Porto do Açu, which eventually bankrupted his companies. In early 2012, Batista had a net worth of US$35 billion, ranking him **the seventh wealthiest person in the world**, and the richest in Brazil. By July 2013, his wealth had plummeted to $200 million due to his debts and his company's falling stock prices. Bloomberg reported in January 2014 that Batista "has a negative net worth." Forbes and Folha de S.Paulo quoted Batista in September 2014, stating that his net worth was –$1 billion. Batista is currently under arrest and has been sentenced to 30 years in prison for bribing disgraced Rio de Janeiro governor Sérgio Cabral, in order to secure public contract.

5

Rules to be Wealthy

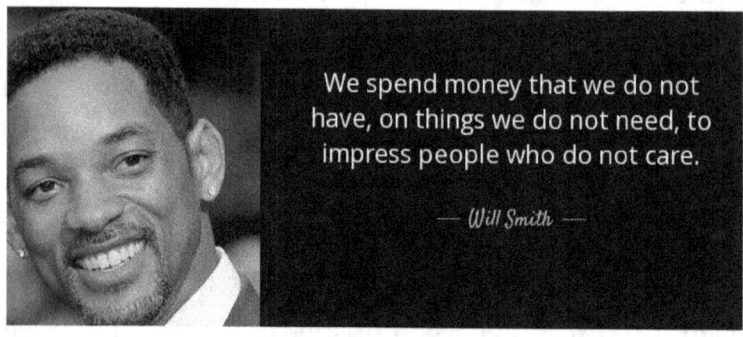

There is no need to drive a luxury car to impress others but cutting your spending as much as you can and learn exactly how much you really need to be comfortable making a habit to save your money regularly and avoid as much as getting into debt and try to manage your asset when enough to get a good return and try to protect your property belongings, Your home should have insurance, take your health because your health is a valuable asset and don't waste your time in that is not productive use, use your time wisely should be knowing why you want to be wealthy and ask yourself what you will do when you will have all the money, how you going to spend time with your family. To create wealth all depend on your behavior and attitude your proportion of a contribution for saving, as you know money does not grow on trees you should be knowing how to invest money wisely and what kind of return you need for your lifestyle to become wealthy. Money cannot make you happy but your freedom to live your life happily the rule is that never borrows money or never asks money as much as you can you should be.

Ben Graham, the father of value investing, used to say that you're not right if other people agree with you you're right if your facts and analysis are right. You must think independently as an investor and this means that at times you must be willing to be different and to stand apart from the crowd. Don't just blindly follow the crowd.

When Warren Buffett thinks he has a good idea, he doesn't just test the water temperature with his toe; he goes all in. This is very rare in the investment world, in which many individuals will take small positions to track certain stocks or won't allow any one stock to comprise more than 10% – or some other arbitrary percentage of their total portfolio. Warren Buffett believes that when you're presented with an opportunity, you must go after it with everything that you have. This means you can't waste time, you must what real success means when you get my age measure your success in life by how many of the people you want to have love you actually to love you that the ultimate test of how you have left the life.

Rules to be Wealthy

Avoid Credit card

Many people spend more than they make and float the difference on credit cards.

Educate yourself

Read about personal finance, education is the single highest correlating factor with income.

Dream bigger

When John D. Rockefeller went into the oil business, in 1863, no one dreamed of freeways. When Google founders Sergey Brin and Larry Page began perfecting online search.

Judge yourself over the year, not the month

While it is important to keep a tab on how you're doing month to month, it's far more important to judge success over longer periods of time

Start Saving

Make more than you spend, and use the excess to invest wisely. How you invest is up to but the obvious goal is to make investments that have a high likelihood of making you more money in the future. That's it. The ways to achieve this are by making more money, spending less, and investing more wisely.

Debt Free

Credit card debt, student debt, and even car loans can carry heavy interest rates that drag you down, demanding monthly instalments that kill away at your revenue while racking up additional interest and penalties that take away even more money from your future self, first-line priority to get rid of your debt as soon as possible.

Diversify your income

Don't rely on one type of investment, and don't gamble all your savings on one venture. Instead, try to set up multiple income streams, generate several backup plans for your goals and businesses.

Work hard

I promise that if you're the first person in the office and the last to leave, you'll get ahead. Pay your dues early and you can relax when you're older.

Live like you're poorer than you actually are

The wealthy you become the more frugal and low-key you should be. Too many young people waste money on things they don't need simply to show off to their friends or on social media.

There's no shame in being young and poor. Drive a cheap car. Live in a modest home. Don't eat out every day. Don't buy clothes you don't need (thanks to Mark Zuckerberg and Steve Jobs, wearing the same thing every day is cool). And then be the unassuming millionaire next door.

Financial Freedom

Money can work for you, and the more of it you employ, the faster and larger it can grow. Along with more money comes more freedom .The freedom to stay home with your kids, the freedom to retire and travel around the world, or the freedom to quit your job. I

Build a portfolio of stocks and shares

If you can make steady investments in stocks over a long period, choose wisely and reinvest the dividends then you can build a large store of wealth. Of course stocks can go either way and many small investors lose heart when their portfolio plunges. But over the long-term, equities are as good an investment as property and much more liquid. Stock market crashes represent great buying opportunities for those with cash and strong nerves.

Cut your expenses

The biggest problem in some people's path of getting rich is that they always spend more than what they earn. Living below your means will be the easiest to get rich.

Consistently track your progress

How much you're spending. Use an app or simply an Excel spreadsheet to make sure you always know how much money you have what where it's going. This gives you a proper place to review and refine what does and doesn't make sense in terms of your spending.

Make investments wisely

Investment is much more than pure luck. One investment mistake could tear away a large chunk of your assets. So make sure whenever you are making decisions on investments, whether on properties or stock, think twice. It will be better for you to consider opinions from professionals and experts.

Financial Budgeting

Have proper financial budgeting and keep under your budget, limit your expenditure and save and invest as per you have designed budget.

6

How to Get Wealthy

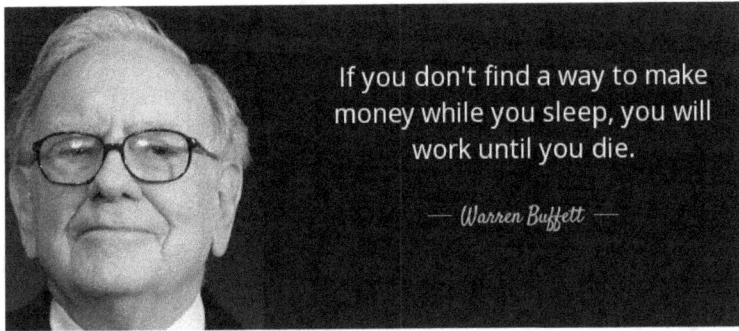

Saving is income not spent or deferred consumption. Methods of saving include putting money aside in, for example, a deposit account, a pension account, an investment fund, or as cash. Saving also involves reducing expenditures, such as recurring costs. In terms of personal finance, saving generally specifies low-risk preservation of money, as in a deposit account, versus investment, wherein risk is a lot higher; in economics more broadly, it refers to any income not used for immediate consumption. Saving does not automatically include interest.

What a person has left over when the cost of his or her consumer expenditure is subtracted from the amount of disposable income earned in a given period of time. Savings can be used to increase income by investing in different investment vehicles.

Savings comprise the amount of money left over after spending. For example, Tommy's monthly pay check is $10,000. Her expenses include a $2,500 rent payment, a $1000 car payment, a $1300 credit card payment, $550 for groceries, $205 for utilities, $175 for her mobile & $ 500 other since his monthly income is $10,000 and her monthly expenses are $6230, Tommy has $3770 leftover.

Saving is important to the economic progress of a country because of its relation to investment. If there is to be an increase in productive wealth, some individuals must be willing to abstain from consuming their entire income. Progress is not dependent on saving alone; there must also be individuals willing to invest and thereby increase productive capacity.

The fact that shouldn't be forgotten is that you need to save for future crises, for the business problems, for travel, for any sort of urgency, for fulfilling a long-cherished dream or for anything.

Investment is, on the other hand, is taking some of your money and trying to make it grow by buying things you think will increase in value. For example, you might invest in stocks, property, or shares in a fund. When investing, it is important to invest wisely. You will have a better return if you begin investing early. Understanding different investment vehicles, what they are for, and how to use them is imperative to being successful. We invest in long term goals, such as our children's college fund or retirement. We use specific vehicles that allow for growth.

The reason to save is to meet the long financial goal through investing. The more you save, the more you will create wealth.

Formula saving and investment

EARN = SAVE - SPEND

Saving is impotant

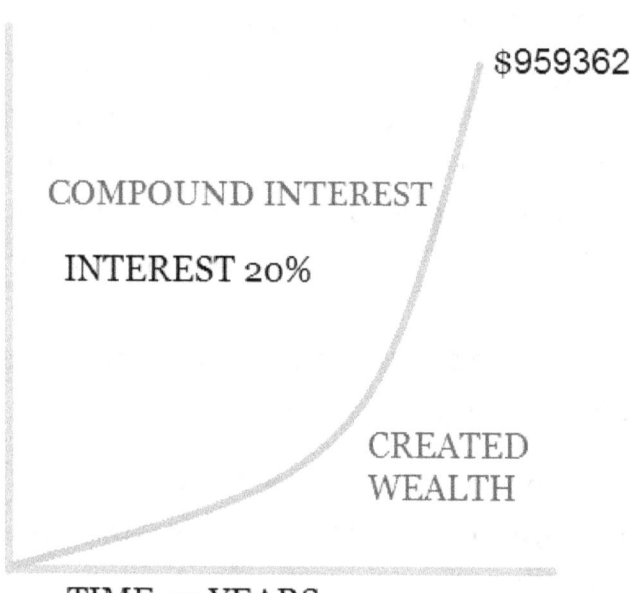

This above graph shows that if you invest $10000 for 25 years @ 20% CAGR, you will be able to create a wealth of $959362.

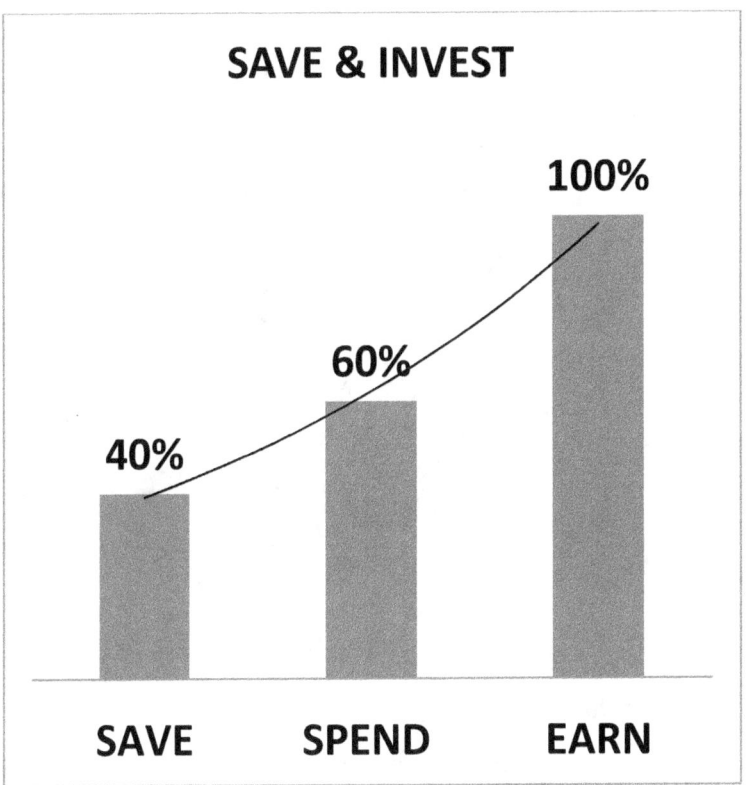

The above graph shows that whatever you earn i.e. if you earn 100%, out of that earning you should be saving at least 40% and rest 60 % you can do your expenditure.

Using this formula, you can start becoming wealthy and will use your money wisely.

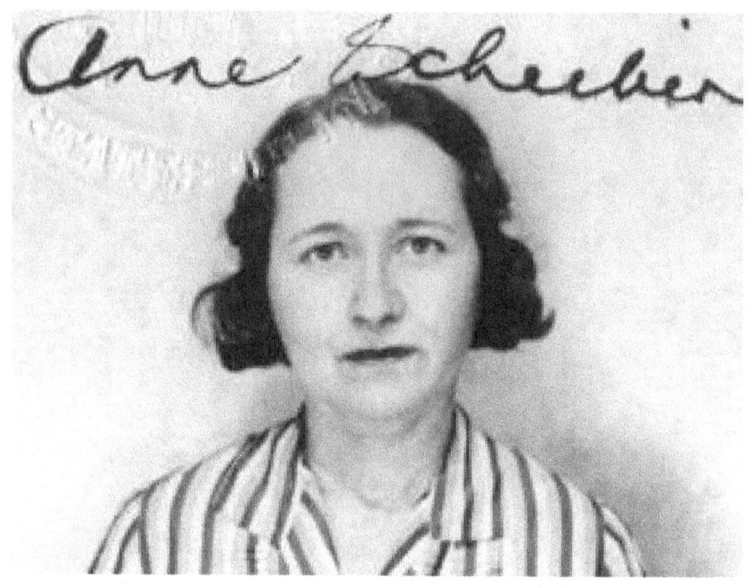

Anne Scheiber was an unknown, reclusive and extremely frugal New York woman who worked as an auditor for the United States Internal Revenue Service, retiring from the IRS in 1944. She never earned a salary of more than $4,000 per year, and although she was an exemplary worker, she never received a promotion. This likely reflected discrimination towards women in the workforce in general during that period, as well as attitudes of anti-Semitism those were endemic in elite American institutions in the mid-20th century, including the U.S. government. Despite her experiences with discrimination, Scheiber's life became noteworthy for her accomplishment as an extremely skillful investor during her 50 years of retirement, and ultimately as a surprise philanthropist in support of women's education. In her early adult years, Scheiber had a series of negative experiences with financial brokers in the 1930s, and eventually retired from her job as an auditor at the IRS in the mid-1940s, with only $5,000 saved up and a $3,100 annual pension. She then spent the next 50 years studying the markets and accumulating wealth while living in her frugal New York apartment. By making a series of wise financial investments, share purchases, and savings, Scheiber managed to accumulate a net worth of $22 ($37.1 million today, when adjusted for inflation) million by the end of her life. Despite her extensive wealth, she had a reputation for frugality and eccentricity, including one incident in which she took food from a meeting of shareholders and consumed it over the next three days. At the end of her life, she lived in the same apartment and wore the same clothing that she did in 1944. After her death in 1995 at the age of 101, she donated her fortune to establishing scholarships for women at Yeshiva University's Stern College for Women, and the Albert Einstein School of Medicine, with the intention of enabling younger women to overcome the discrimination that she herself had endured during her working years. Her gift shocked and surprised many, not only for its size but that its source came from a donor who was unknown and lived in virtual obscurity.

Anne Scheiber Portfolio.

Company (symbol)	No. of shares owned	Dec. 11 price	1995 gain
SCHERING-PLOUGH (sgp)	64,000	$59.25	62%
PEPSICO (pep)	27,000	57.50	65
ALLIED SIGNAL (ald)	20,934	49.25	44
LOEWS (ltr)	14,061	78.00	75
BRISTOL-MYERS SQUIBB (bmy)	10,080	84.50	45
COCA-COLA (ko)	9,048	79.25	60
ALLEGHENY POWER SYSTEM (ayp)	8,000	28.25	30
ROCKWELL INTERNATIONAL (rok)	4,640	51.75	46
UNOCAL (ucl)	3,690	28.75	10
EXXON (xon)	1,664	84.00	39

Secret millionaires like Scheiber often owe their riches to value investing, dividend investing, and passive investing. Such investors tend to focus on long-term ownership with low turnover, reasonable costs, and tax efficiency, abandoning things like market timing and focusing on fundamentals instead.

Anne Scheiber's story is worth emulating if you want financial independence. Her example strengthens the argument that with a long compounding period and prudent decisions, capital tends to flourish. For anyone interested in putting their money to work for many decades, Scheiber's story is worth examining.

Scheiber had the knowledge, experience, time, and desire to analyze the underlying economics of stocks, bonds, and other assets. This gave her peace of mind when markets collapsed, many times over her investing career, stocks declined by 33% to 50% because she knew what she owned and why she owned it. She understood how the earnings and cash flow were generated, and that relative to the price she paid, she was still likely to experience a satisfactory outcome if she held on no matter how bad it looked at the time.

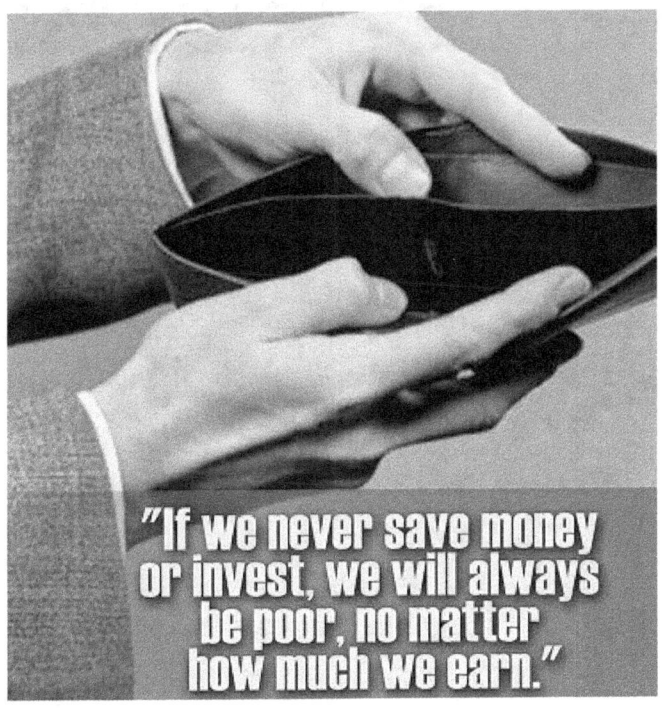

"If we never save money or invest, we will always be poor, no matter how much we earn."

7

Leverage

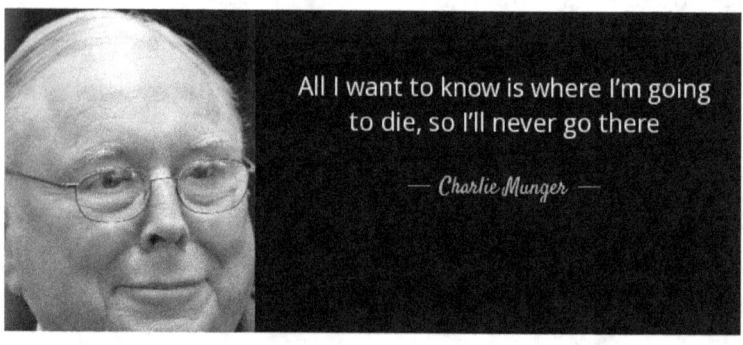

When you combine ignorance and leverage, you get some pretty interesting results. *"I've seen more people fail because of liquor and leverage – leverage being borrowed money. You really don't need leverage in this world much. If you're smart, you're going to make a lot of money without borrowing."*

-Warren buffett

Avoiding debt requires you to establish a sound financial plan. Individuals who face financial difficulties and seem to be accumulating more debt instead of taking control of their finances. If you are getting deeper into debt financial knowledge maybe they can help you get your finances back on track again. In today's world young people are using debt to live what they think is an easy life, buying unnecessary items to keep up with the latest trends, partying, and switching from credit card to credit card to pay off racked up bills. In my opinion, young people lack the knowledge, and understanding of how credit works, and what it takes to keep up with the responsibilities of owning a credit card.

Leverage is to multiple their buying power in the market .when you take leverage to make more money but there is a reason behind leverage, there also can be a loss that you pay the cost of borrowing and some time is done to be the face of bankruptcy defaulter payment, using leverage you can buy your house, buy a new car and then you pay the interest to bank and the lenders are ready to find you monthly payment limit amount of money you have to spend on the other things.

The best we can see the credit card, auto loan, student loan that are easy we get but we have to pay but in case you could not able to make a payment , you may stress that can lead to mild to your health problem during ulcer, migraine, depression, and heart attack. It can affect your credit score. Leverage makes happy it is just a psychological way to mark.

8

Financial Freedom

FINANCIAL FREEDOM = WHEN YOU NO LONGER HAVE TO WORRY ABOUT MONEY

"What then is freedom? The power to live as one wishes."

— Marcus Tullius Cicero

Financial independence is the status of having enough income to pay one's living expenses for the rest of one's life without having to be employed or dependent on others. Income earned without having to work a job is commonly referred to as passive income.

Financial freedom is a goal for every human being freedom means you have enough money so that you can afford your lifestyle to have enough money you should first save invest properly, To enjoy financial freedom once must follow financial blueprint, make a budget to cover all your financial, need pay off your credit card or any loan, read a book about the personal finance meet financial advisors & start investing and important is to live below your means be frugal when possible and always take care of your belongings take care of yourself and stay healthy and you should always set a life goal what you want from your life. what kind of decision you will take today will going to create your beautiful tomorrow, make a proper budget , your monthly budget your bills to be paid on time pay off your credit card avoid taking much that. And you think positive about the money being think positive for the money will affect opportunities and open more than you ever thought possible.

You should always write your goals and always try to read. Your goal is the reflection of your financial freedom. You should always plan every day in advance so that you can able to control your track and spending habits as well stop first all you need to invest in yourself you need to start reading good books about the personal finance and find about how money works, in short, we can say that financial freedom is allow you to live your life as you want. You will have time for your passion to enjoy financial freedom. what kind of savings you are doing today we should have a complete list of mortgage car loan credit card any kind of loan any kind of money that you have borrowed from your friend you should pay first and then you should have a list of your all stocks what you are holding, what kind of investment you have done and what are the returned your getting. You should be writing them all your goals nearby years whose goal is for the short term and for the long-term. What your plan for retirement, how much money required being financially free, that goal should be very clearly written by yourself.

In writing a goal you can understand current facts by asking yourself. When I can achieve this goal? How long it will take? spending less today can change my life tomorrow like the example of Warren Buffett who have to purchase a home in 1958 $31500 and till today is life in the same house, Warren Buffett net worth more than 88 billion dollars so he can always afford a bigger than expensive house and cars but his locality might very well be the reason why is one of the world's richest person.

Basic Calculation to be financially Free and enjoy Financial Freedom

25 Multiple Rule to be financially free.

Financial Freedom

ANNUAL LIVING EXPENSES $ 100000

TO RETIRE CORPUS   25 X $100000

TOTAL RETIRE CORPUS $2500000 ($2.5 Million)

RETIREMENT WITHDRAWAL RATE   5%

RETUIREMENT FUND REQUIRE FROM 2.5 Million @ 5% EACH YEAR = $125000

Above example state that Bill has an annual income of $100000 and he wants to be financially free and come out of the rat race, he wants to live his passion so if you use 25 X to find out how much Bill requires to be free, total Retire Fund Bill require is $2.5 Million and, he can invest or he can save and out of this $2.5 Million, if he withdraws 5 % as we have taken example, Bill can get home $125000, which is above his annual income, what Bill is earning currently. Even you can use the same blueprint to be financially free and enjoy financial freedom.

You should always save and invest in your future for your rainy days for your retirement in case you die to help ensure your family doesn't draw pain for your funeral .You should always save your money for a six-month emergency fund and making sure that money is spent on things that you really need like food shelter so taking a look and those finance building additional stream of income payload pay down the death and before you know it you will be free.

Financial freedom mean that you should not be living pay check to pay check but the reality is that millions of people are living pay check to pay check today and they really don't know what is financial freedom, you must have enough money to quit your job it is just a feeling that you are in a zoo, quit your job and you can have enough time to be financially happy and doing what you enjoy your life as living and follow your passion and spend more time with your family and not going completely broke. You must be having enough money actually to retire compare to many other people who retired but still not able to live a very happy life not having enough to get a dream retirement follow the passions due to the financial burden because they have never understand how to save money and how many times you dream about getting your boring 9 to 5 job and to live life unification living life to the fullest and financial freedom is about much more than just having money it is the freedom to be who you really are and what you really want in life , it's about following your passion in charge that can influence by living life to your terms if you want to be fine and you need to become a different person than you are today and let go of whatever and hurt you bad in the past and you need to think about your power your happiness as like a butterfly shading is born and achievement of your dream , I think that is a true for the financial freedom when you do know that the death is going to kill you why you need to borrow date and to become a slave of the death you can never enjoy the connection freedom if you have a lots of death. Financial freedom is a journey it is not a destination. Financial freedom means many different things to different people as a person gets older they realize that I need to spend more time with family and friends and things they enjoy things you wish to do.

Importance of money is just seeing the family get up and have debts problem money can create unnecessary stress depression in a daily life.

Freedom means that you don't have to work hard for money, living expenses should meet by passive income generated by your as much equal or exceed your least your daily expenses Why so financial freedom is so important you can live your life independently having time for the picnic you can spend time with your kids you don't have to worry about vegetables you will be having enough time for the volunteers for causes you care about you will be having time to know your children what to provide them and at last you should have a sound sleep and you are not worried about your financial situations. And you know the future is uncertain we should always do proper planning.

9

Power of Investing

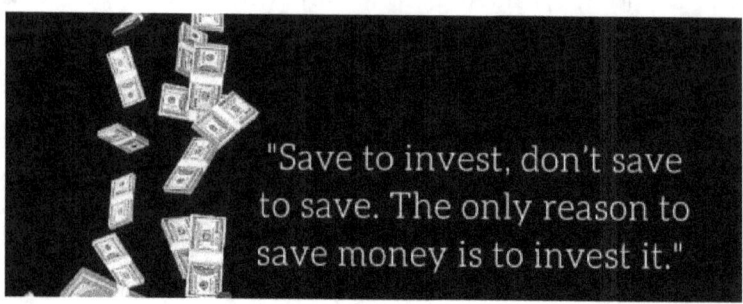

"Save to invest, don't save to save. The only reason to save money is to invest it."

The snowball just happens if you're in the right kind of snow, and that's what happened with me. I don't just mean compounding money either. It's in terms of understanding the world and what kind of friends you accumulate. You get to select over time, and you've got to be the kind of person that the snow wants to attach itself to. **You've got to be your own wet snow, in effect. You'd better be picking up snow as you go along, because you're not going to be getting back up to the top of the hill again. That's the way life works.**
-Warren Buffett

The Story of Compound Interest

The king was pleased. He had every reason to feel this way. One of his subjects had invented a sport that had become his new favourite pastime. The game went by the name of chess.

The inventor was asked to appear before the king. The generous king asked the inventor to name his reward. Anything the inventor desired.

The inventor's answer shocked the king.

"I am a simple man of few wants, he said. My needs are a few. Give me one grain of rice for the first square of the chessboard, two for the second, four for the third and so on. Each square having double the number of rice than the previous square. This is all I ask of thee, O generous king."

The king was offended. Here he was, a mighty emperor, asking this peasant to ask him for anything he desired and all he was asking for was a few grains of rice. Surely this was an affront!

"I mean thee no disrespect O mighty king. This is all my heart desires and all that I need."

The king calmed down. He ordered his minister,

"Give this fool what he wants and let us be done with his request. Take him out of my sight"

A week passed. Still no sign of the minister. He was asked to appear before the king immediately.

"Explain your absence", said the irritated king.

"We are still trying to procure the required number of rice to fill the chessboard, your majesty. We have sent people far and wide to collect rice but we still haven't been able to procure enough rice"

The minister should not have even bothered. The required amount of rice has not been produced in the history of mankind.

For the mathematically inclined, the number of grains of rice required to fill the chess board is 18,446,744,073,709,551,615.

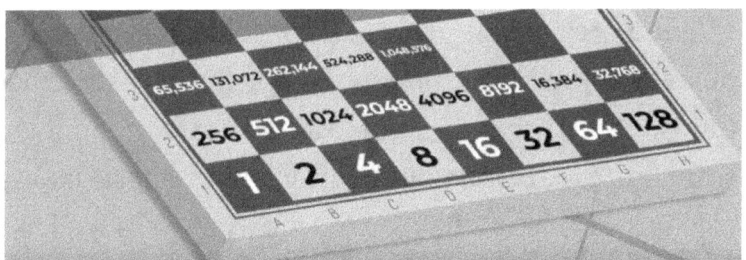

The power of compound interest.

Investing at any age isn't easy, but waiting to invest for when it's convenient isn't the best approach either as there will never be a perfect time to start. You don't need to wait for that large lump sum or that perfect timing in the markets to take the plunge. Start as early as you can, with an amount you can afford, even if it's just $100, and then build it up gradually. The sooner you put your dollars to work, the more likely you are to benefit in the long term. Putting it off could actually cost you more than you realize.

Would you rather have 1 million dollars today or a penny that doubled every day for 30 days? Without hesitation, some people would say $1 million of course! However, the "correct" answer would have been the compounding penny over the course of 30 days, which results in over $5 million dollars.

The goal of investing is to build wealth over time and to generate income from your investments to meet objectives. Investors purchase assets such as mutual funds, stocks, bonds, real estate and commodities with the expectation that the value of these assets will increase and that their financial goals will be realized. Successful investing requires time, patience and a clear and realistic plan directed toward your goal.

This Process require for Investing

Time Horizon

The more time you have to build wealth, the more potential there is to reach your goals.

Rate of Return

Investors can seek higher return potential over time for taking more risk. Rate of return is required as per the investor willing to take the risk.

Amount Invested

What amount invested is willing to invest .The power of investing is the most powerful force of the universe that the principle of compounding, In other words, if you have $500 and earn 10% in interest, you have $550. Then, if you earn 10% of interest on that, you end up with $605. And so on, until eventually, your original $500 is eclipsed by the amount of interest you have gained. The power of investing in stock that to make profit from the capital gain.

The foundation behind compounding interest is the concept of the time values of money, which states that, the value of money changes depending upon when it is received. Having $100 today is preferable to receiving it a years' time from now because you can invest it to generate dividends and interest income. Compounding interest allows that money to grow. By postponing the receipt of the $100, your opportunity cost grows.

Opportunity cost is the loss of possible gains if an action is not chosen in this case, the amount of money you do not receive if you take no action with it. If you did not invest the $500, you have lost the opportunity to earn $50 you could have gained in a year. In 10 years, your $500 would have been $1,427; you have lost the opportunity to gain $927 by not investing the money.

The best way to understand these concepts is to put them into a compound interest table that shows you just how substantially your wealth can multiply over time.

Imagine you have an investor who sets aside a lump sum of $10,000. Take a look at the compound interest chart to see the influence of time and rate of return on his ultimate wealth.

Once you understand this, it becomes evident that saving money alone is not the key to a large fortune.

Compound Interest Chart

	4%	8%	12%	16%
10 Years	$14,802	$21,589	$31,058	$44,114
20 Years	$21,911	$46,610	$96,463	$194,608
30 Years	$32,434	$100,627	$299,600	$858,500
40 Years	$48,010	$217,245	$930,510	$3,787,212
50 Years	$71,067	$469,016	$2,890,022	$16,707,038

When people think of interest, they often think of debt. But interest can work in your favour when you're earning it on money you've saved and invested.

Compound interest can be defined as interest calculated on the initial principal and also on the accumulated interest of previous periods. Think of it as the cycle of earning "interest on interest" which can cause wealth to rapidly snowball. Compound Interest will make a deposit or loan grow at a faster rate than simple interest, which is interest calculated only on the principal amount.

Investment or investing is not a gambling there are but this is a calculated risk taking you are investing money for a long term in order to gain a financial return

The earlier you start investing, the bigger the payoff. Use compound interest "Compound interest is the most powerful force in the universe." He called it "the eighth wonder of the world" and "the greatest mathematical discovery of all time." Compound interest is simply defined as interest being earned on interest. It can transform a small amount of money into a high-powered, income-generating machine.

The two key ingredients for compounding to be effective are the reinvestment of earnings and time.

The younger you are the more able and willing you is to take risks on your investments. This is because you have many productive earning years ahead of you to grow your wealth.

Use financial markets over the last century; the stock market's average return is about 10% annually.

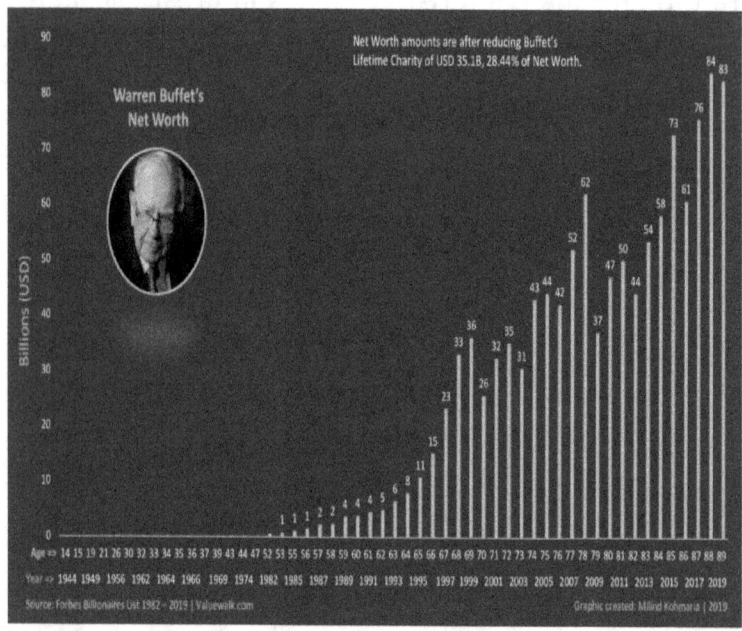

Warren Buffett investing journey

Below example of two friends Age 25 and 35 year, both invested and there return.

When beginning to invest, the person is...	25 years old	35 years old
Each person invest $100/month for...	10 years	30 years
With an 8 percent rate of return, at age 65 their accounts are worth...	$200,061. Voilà – the value of starting early	$149,036. Even though he invested for three times as long, he's behind by $50,000

The above example state that both invested the same amount of $100 month but there is a time difference of 10 years, where one who started early with 8% for age 65 created $200061 vs. after 10 years started investing created $ 143036. This example shows the early you invest, the more you create wealth.

Skipping Coffree cappuccino Can Get You Over $800,000.

Take, for instance, a daily $5 cappuccino from Starbucks. If you were to skip the cappuccino and instead invest that $5 a day in the stock market, your coffee fund could grow to almost $11,000 in 5 years. Keep investing $5 a day for 50 years, and you could have more than $800,000 – just by making coffee at home.

Investing $5 to Become a Millionaire

Investing Early to be Successful

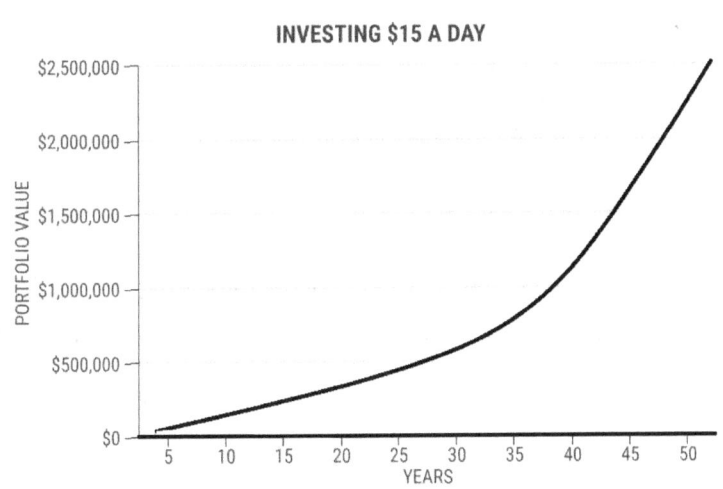

An investor who put $15 a day into the stock market could grow her portfolio to more than $1.2 million in 40 years. If she kept investing $15 a day for 50 years, she could almost $2.5 million.

Invest Early

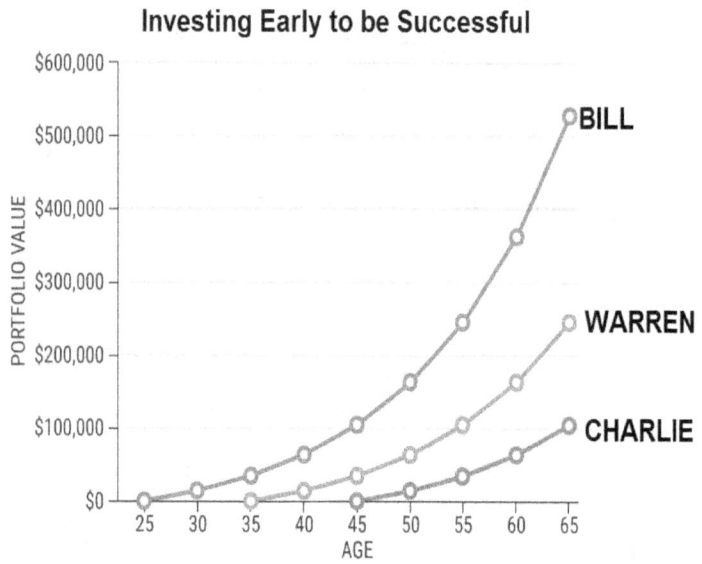

The stock market is kindest to those who stay faithful to it longest. To see this, consider investors Bill, Warren and Charlie. Bill starts investing $200 per month when he's 25. By age 65, his portfolio is worth more than $520,000.

Warren doesn't start investing until age 35. He also contributes $200 per month, but by 65, her portfolio is only worth about $245,000. By waiting ten years to start, He ends up with less than half what bill accumulates. Charlie, the late bloomer, starts investing $200 per month when he's 45 and after 20 years has only $100,000.

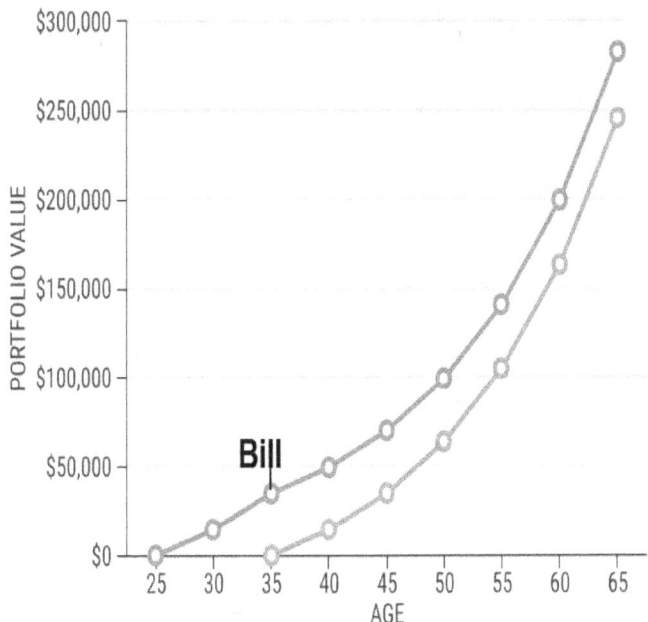

Time invested is so important that Bill can even stop adding to his investments and still have more than Warren at age 65.

If Bill were to contribute $200 per month from age 25 to 35 - contributing only $24,000 in total over 10 years - his investments would be worth almost $300,000 at age 65. Warren continually invests $200 per month between ages 35 and 65 but still ends up with only $245,000 at 65. Even though he contributes three times as much as Bill over her lifetime ($72,000), because he missed those first 10 years of investing.

Financial Freedom to be with Investing

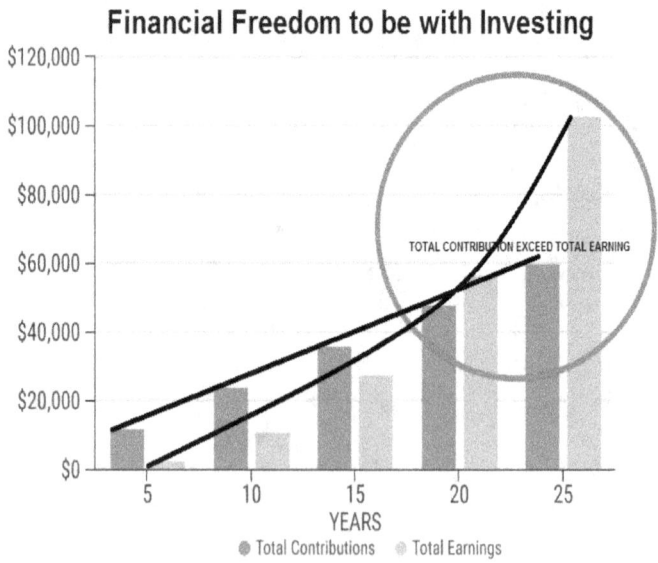

Bill earnings will grow so large; they'll exceed all of his contributions combined. After 20 years of investing, Bill contributed $48,000 in total. That same year, his $48,000 earned over $56,000. By year 25, his earnings $103,000 are over 70 percent larger than his total contributions $60,000.

This is why time is so important in investing: Given enough time, your earnings can compound to take on a life of their own. Even better are they can become self-sustainable. When your money is earning enough money that you no longer need to work, you've achieved financial independence.

$200 Become $1Million

After five years of investing $200 per month at a 7 percent return, you'd have put in $12,000 and only earned $2,400. But over time, those earnings compound until the amount you contribute looks paltry in comparison to your returns.

If you keep investing that $200 every month until age 70, for instance, you'll have contributed $120,000 but could have amassed almost $976,000 in earnings for a total portfolio of $1.1 million

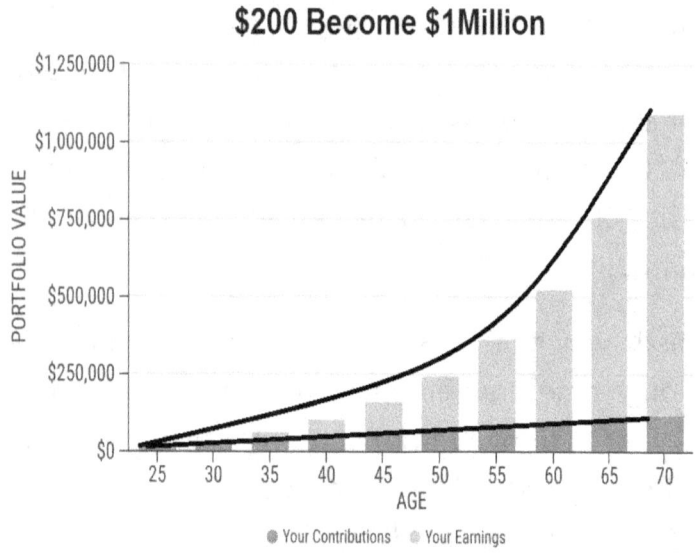

Investing means to use your money to make more money. Technically, anything that generates a return is an "investment". This means even your savings account generating 1% interest is an "investment". However, when most people talk about investing, they are referring to higher return investments like mutual funds, ETFs, and stocks.

Investing ensures present and future long-term financial security. The money generated from your investments can provide financial security and income.

One of the ways investments like stocks, bonds, and ETFs provide income is by way of a dividend. This is an amount paid to shareholders simply for holding the investment. Because many investments pay monthly, quarterly, or annual distributions, you can enjoy a passive income that ultimately could replace your paycheque.

In today's world, just earning money is not enough. You work hard for the money you earn. But that may not be adequate for you to lead a comfortable lifestyle or fulfil your dreams and goals. To do that, you need to make your money work hard for you as well. This is why you invest. Money lying idle in your bank account is an opportunity lost. You should invest that money smartly to get good returns out of it.

The emphasis here is on today for tomorrow. To explain this further, you definitely have a today to spend on and the expenses to cover, these expenses may include house exp (miscellaneous ones) expenses for your child's education also other activities, your own expenses, your spouse's expenses, etc. These expenses actually never end. But then, you are earning today tomorrow you will not be earning, what about your tomorrow? What about your child's higher studies? What about an emergency, an unforeseen event? There are so many questions unanswered, so much that you need to answer, yet you have not investments for your future.

10

Income Type

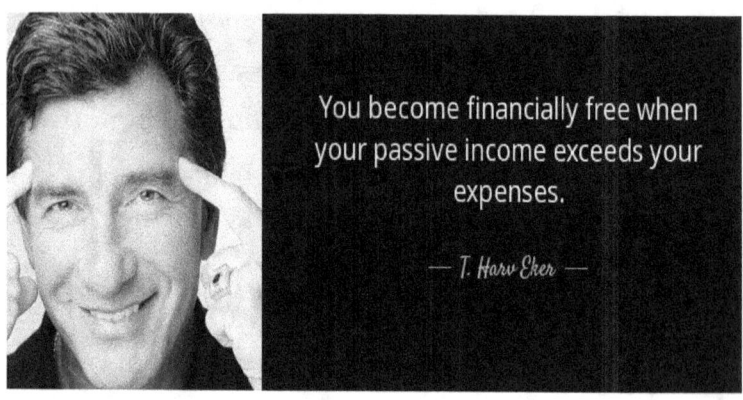

Before I dive into the reasons why passive income is so important, let's first describe what it actually is. Passive income is income that's received automatically with little requirement for maintenance. In contrast, active income can only be earned by directly translating your time for money. Whether it's a pay-per-hour job or a salaried one, the amount of money you make is directly correlated to your time.

With active income, when you don't work, you can't earn. If something were to happen to you and you were incapacitated for whatever reason through an injury, illness or some other calamity, you would lose your ability to earn. If, for example, you were an athlete and you injured yourself so badly that you were unable to continue your occupation, you would lose your ability to compete and earn money altogether.

If you work as a contractor or a builder, without mobility and the usage of all your limbs, how could you work? If something were to happen to you and you lost a leg or an arm, how could you continue to earn money? If you got sick and needed an organ transplant and were out of work for months, how long do you think your employer would keep you on before letting you go? If your car broke down and you didn't have money to fix it, how could you go show homes as a realtor or meet with prospective clients in any other capacity? It would certainly become far more difficult.

Most of the world lives in accordance to an active-income credo. They earn only based on the time that they work. The wealthy, however, operate on another set of standards, which involve a detachment of their physical time for the money that they earn. They earn passive income from a number of sources such as real estate rentals, dividends, interest income, royalties, franchise frees, website advertisements and so on.

Now, don't get me wrong. Creating a passive income stream is a massive undertaking. It involves the investment of a tremendous amount of time. During that investment of time, you receive no income. You're investing your time with the hopes of producing an income down the road, not today. With active income, the money you earn is directly correlated to the time you work. But passive income continues to pay you long after the work has been completed.

Clearly, there are a number of ways to make passive income. Whether you're looking to make money online or simply earn passive income through more traditional means such as real estate rentals, there are a number of ways to produce these types of income streams. While difficult at first, what you'll come to realize is not only the importance of having passive income in your life, but you'll also become addicted to it, seeking out ways to produce additional streams of this powerful fiscal method.

So when it comes down to it, there are likely dozens of reasons why having passive income is important in your life. This doesn't mean that you have to quit your active-income employment. Of course, if you can afford to do that and throw yourself at passive-income generation, then you'll fare much better down the road. But many people simply can't afford to do that. With debt and other financial obligations, going without income for a specific period is simply not

Type of Income

Active income

Passive income

We should understand what exactly the income is; income is divided in two parts Active & Passive. we will go through the passive income strategy from this book will going to learn how to use a passive income strategy to generate higher income to meet a requirement of a financial goals compare to active income from which service has been performed including wages and salaries Commission income from business where in compared to the passive income earning and individual from rental property or dividend or share investment Only working for it another word we can see money on by smart working.

Income that is generates s from a source other than an employer or contractor.

ACTIVE INCOME	PASSIVE INCOME
1 MONTHLY PAYCHECK	1 RENTAL INCOME
2 BUSINESS PROFIT	2 DEVIDEND INCOME
3 PROFESSIONAL FEE	3 FIXED DEPOSIT INTEREST
4 BONUS	4 ROYALTY INCOME
5 SALES COMMISSION	5 CAPITAL GAIN INCOME

Active income

Income earned from an exchange of physical labour, Income earned by doing something or by spending your time e.g. the money that you make in your job, the salary you get by working for someone else. Now, this is where your quality of life will suffer the most, because you will be trading your time for money. In most cases, jobs will pay you just enough to stay over broke. Quite obviously job means Just over broke. Now, the reason why most people are not able to think beyond earning money through a job is because Job will provide you with a 'relatively' comfortable zone.

Unfortunately, this comfort zone will become your biggest enemy and will keep you away from leading an extraordinary life. You will spend the maximum time of your life in this income stream and still will never have enough money to lead a truly wealthy life.

"Comfort is your biggest trap and coming out of comfort zone your biggest enemy" ~ From the Rat Race to Financial Freedom

Income for which services have been performed. This includes wages, tips, salaries, commissions, and income from businesses in which there is material participation

Passive income

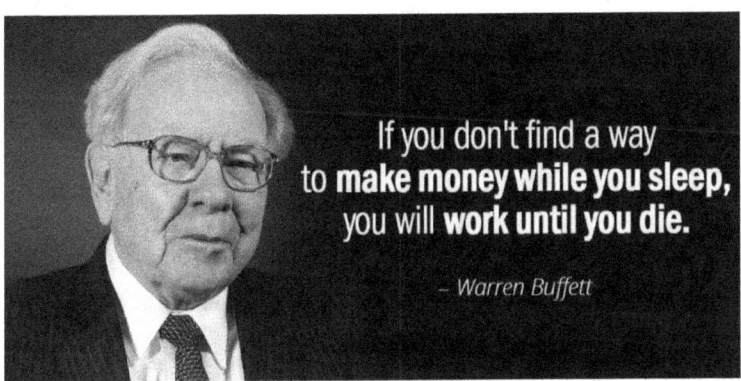

Warren buffett earn At Coke's current quarterly payout of $0.40 per share, Berkshire's 400 million

shares will bring in $640 million over the next year in dividend income. Since 1995, it has earned about $7 billion in dividends from the Coke investment.

Income Generated from different sources

- Interest from fixed deposit, P2P lending and other forms of lending.
- Coupons from bonds.
- Dividend from stocks.
- Rental income from property.
- Royalty from intellectual property.
- Owning businesses that you don't physically manage.

Money that you earn by selling something for more than it costs you to make. e.g. Businesses selling their goods at a profit, whether at the retail or wholesale level, as distributors or manufacturers. You need to be an entrepreneur for earning profits. You might need huge investments or you could start a small business for profit with small investments too. But this will also take away a lot of your time, at least in the initial stages - until you learn to manage it really well and be able to make it churn of its own. Entrepreneurship is a different kind of mindset and risk taking capability.

Most of the people who are in job and are used to the 'Earned Income' want to move to this category at some stage of their career or life, but find it difficult to make the move - primarily because of lack of guts to take additional risks. Most often, this lack of courage is justified because of the family constraints and needs. To be an entrepreneur and start earning profits, you will need to identify a product or a service that you want to sell, and then sell and manage it well, and manage your clients equally well.

For most people, 'Earned Income' and 'Profit Income' 'Interest Income' money you get as a result of lending your money to someone else to use, e.g. putting it in the bank, lending it to the government in the form of buying Treasury Bills etc.

This is a great source of passive income where your active involvement is not needed once the investment is done. Many doubt on the seriousness of wealth 'Interest Income' can generate, but when combined with the power of compounding, and the fact that this is a true passive income with least amount of risk.

Dividend Income This income gets even better than Interest Income. It is equally passive and not only that, it also makes you a shareholder of a company. This is the money that you get as a return on shares of a company you own. If you invest smartly on ex-dividend dates of good blue chip companies, you can far exceed the returns from Dividend Income than what you get from the Interest Income, since you are also a party to the Capital Gains that the share price goes through. This is one of the key instruments that we recommend for generating adequate Cash Flow and still get very good income. Shareholders in companies with dividend-yielding stocks receive a payment at regular intervals from the company. Companies pay cash dividends on a quarterly basis out of their profits, and all you need to do is own the stock. Dividends are paid per share of stock, so the more shares you own, the higher and your payout. Since the income from the stocks isn't related to any activity other than the initial financial investment, owning dividend-yielding stocks can be one of the most passive forms of making money.

Rental Income this is the money that you get as a result of renting out an asset that you have, like a house, or a building. One of the biggest drawbacks is the amount of money required to create such an asset which can generate regular rental income. Since the money required is huge, you may not be able to create many such assets in your life time, unless you have other sources of income.

Royalty Income this is the money you get as a result of letting someone use your products, ideas, or processes. They make all the revenues, they do all the hard work and you get a small percentage of whatever they earn.

Most types of passive income are derived from real estate/property, while other types of passive income are derived from royalties from patents or license agreements.

"Many people think that passive income is about getting something for nothing," Tresidder says. *"It has* a 'get-rich-quick' appeal ... but in the end, it still involves work. You just give the work upfront."

"Don't let making a living prevent you from making a life." — John Wooden

Time is precious. It's sacred. Just 24 hours in a day. That's all we get. Not one person on this earth has more time than that. No matter their age, occupation, religion, color of their skin or where they live. No one. Time is the greatest equalizer because not a single person can have more of it. It can never be recreated or re-spent. It exists once, and then it's gone. And that's precisely why passive income is so important because time is more valuable than money.

Unlike money, which can be earned, saved, spent, invested, squandered and lost, we can't tuck away minutes on a clock. We can't expect dividends on seconds or hours in the bank, or invest the time that we didn't use on something else. Considering that most of the free world needs to work for a living, consuming much of the time they do have, this precious commodity needs to be nurtured and savoured.

Passive income is quite possibly one of the most important and central ways that the rich get richer.

It's how you detach your ability to earn from the time that you do have in a day. If you've ever heard the term, making money while you sleep, no truer words have been spoken. With passive income, you do make money while you sleep. You also make money while you're awake. It's automatic and simply keeps coming in.

However, creating a passive income stream is far from automatic. It's no easy feat by any measure. It takes an enormous amount of effort and exertion of your time with very little return in the beginning. It involves an overall sense of frustration and an enormous learning curve. Still, it's one of the most fruitful and worthwhile investments of your time that you could possibly engage in.

While passive income might not be the answer to all of your immediate problems, it is the pathway to success and most certainly the foundation for wealth and happiness. When you're not stressed just to make enough money to pay the bills and you're no longer living from paycheck-to-paycheck, there's a mental clarity and an emotional catharsis that sets in. You become free from the shackles of a life-sucking 9-to-5 job and begin embracing a more fulfilled life.

When you have the time to choose to work or spend those precious moments with your children or go on some trip halfway around the world, you're free. You're free in the greatest sense of the word. Aren't all the headache and the hassle worth that? Isn't it time to break the chains that have restrained you to a life that's been less fulfilled? I would think so. And I would imagine that if you truly are serious about getting wealthy in life, then you'll embrace the passive-income machine.

Passive Income Is so Important

All things considered, time is our greatest asset. In fact, time is far more valuable than money. While money can be spent and earned, time can only be used up but just once. After that time has passed, it's gone forever. You can never physically relive that moment again. This is why passive income is so important because it gives you the freedom of time. When you're less shackled by the necessity to earn just to meet your monthly financial obligations, you have the freedom of time.

This doesn't mean you have total freedom from all of life's obligations; it simply means that you have the flexibility that comes along with not having to struggle to make ends meet at the end of the month. As long as you can ensure that your passive income outpaces your monthly expenses, you're free to spend your time as you choose. With each new passive income stream, your revenue eventually far surpasses your expenses and you ultimately attain true financial freedom.

When you have freedom of time because you're not engaged in active income work, you're free to do as you please. You can choose to travel the world and become a digital nomad. You can choose to settle down and start a family. You can engage in work related to creating additional passive-income streams of revenue. The choice is yours. You have the freedom to choose because you have the freedom of time. That's the power of passive income.

It reduces your stress, anxiety and fear of the future there's nothing worse than having the pressure that comes along with an inability to pay your bills. It causes anxiety, fear and an overall hopeless desperation for the future. The what if scenarios begin to encircle your mind, like a hawk flying above its prey prior to swooping in for the kill. It does a number on you mentally, physically and spiritually. It emotionally beats you up and destroys your hopes and aspirations.

Anytime we live in dire fear of the future, it's hard to be present. It's hard to enjoy what we have in the here-and-now because we're so tied up with those doomsday scenarios. We're so worried about an impending fiscal collapse that it's hard to extricate ourselves from the shackles of that train of thought. It consumes and becomes you. It's hard to get away from that when it's all you can think about.

Passive income helps to alleviate all of these worries. It helps to put fears to bed because you aren't worried about losing your job or being the by-product of corporate-downsizing. When you don't have to worry so much about impending financial doom, not only do you feel better mentally and emotionally, but it translates into physical vitality. You have more energy and are more motivated to get out there and achieve more because passive income also helps to build that all-important financial momentum in life.

It allows you to pursue doing the things you love rather than what pays the bills .We all have things that we're passionate about doing in life. But we always seem to put them off for later. Whether it's art or music or travel, we can indulge our fantasies when passive income frees us from debt that tethers us to the never-ending cycle of payments and interest. It allows you to exit that proverbial rat race by elevating you above all the things that worry so-called "normal folks."

It also frees you to produce an active income by following your heart. When your passive income outpaces your debts, maybe you want to help out at a homeless shelter downtown that can't pay you and they can't pay you much. Whatever it is, you can do it because you're not worried about the pay check.

It doesn't matter what you're passionate about, you can do it. If you want to take a language class for a few weeks and study full time, you can. When you want to go camping with your kids for a full week, you can. You don't need to worry about calling in sick or taking time off from work. You're your own boss. It's the dream of those out there that wake up every single day dreading another moment of work that totally and utterly bores them.

It gives you the ability to live and work from anywhere. I don't know about you, but I have a deep-down passion for travel. If I were to categorize the things in this world that I love the most as a pastime, that would be amongst one of the top contenders. But the problem with travel, for most people, is that it's temporary. It's a momentary state of bliss that seems to come and go too fast. But this isn't about just taking a week-or-two vacation from work; this is about really travelling the world with the ability to work (or not) from any place.

Still, it's easy to not put passive income as a priority when you're so actively concerned about the day-to-day. Rising above that is difficult. But you just need to set a goal, focus and move towards that goal with persistent action on a daily basis. There is light at the end of the tunnel. It will take your time, but you'll eventually get there. It all just depends on how badly you want it and how important it is to you at the end of the day.

It provides a platform for financial stability and growth, when your income is automatic, and you don't need to worry about meeting your expenses at the end of the month by exchanging your direct time for money, it allows you to think and explore new ways to further strengthen your financial stability, and to grow it. It gives you the time to research things like taxes, stocks and other investments. This helps to create fiscal clarity in your mind, fueling you towards your financial goals.

It's easier to train your focus on your finances when you're not pulled in so many other directions. While problems can and still will arise in your life, financially and otherwise, you'll be better prepared to deal with them. Without having the obligation of rushing off to a job you dread every single day, you can train your mind's eye on the things that will provide you with greater growth and prosperity over time.

No matter how you look at it, the importance of passive income is paramount. Many people discount it because they either don't understand it or don't think that having passive income that exceeds your expenses isn't an attainable goal. Well, whatever the mind believes, the mind can achieve. That's as true for passive income as it is for anything else in life. Believe it wholeheartedly with your spirit, and you can accomplish it. As long as you don't give up.

11

Power of Stock Investing

Berkshire, which owns everything from GEICO to Fruit of the Loom to Dairy Queen, and is a major investor in dozens of other stocks, has returned an annual average return of 20.5% since it began trading in 1965.

Stock and any kind of investment it has been through by the value investor who have made millions of dollar in stock investing the legendary value investor that every investor look up to create wealth. By investing in a good stock and holding them for a long. Focus on understanding the underline of the company to invest in that and to wait for the stock to appreciate the value.

"Successful Investing takes time, discipline and patience. No matter how great the talent or effort, some things just take time: You can't produce a baby in one month by getting nine women pregnant." – Warren Buffett

Inflation is not your friend when you're trying to save for a major outlay, like buying a house or financing a comfortable retirement. Consider that the historical inflation rate in the United States hovers at around 3 percent. Then think about how this could eat into the purchasing power of money that's sitting in a certificate of deposit (CD) or savings account. It would have to earn at least 3 percent just to keep up with inflation, and even high-yield savings accounts don't offer much over 2 percent.

If you decide to invest in stocks to grow your wealth, understand that there's no guarantee of how your stocks will perform. Still, it's not necessary to buy stock in the next Amazon or Apple to earn a respectable return: Consider that the stock market has averaged a 10 percent annual return on investments since 1926, as measured by the S&P 500.

"The best way to measure your investing success is not by whether you're beating the market but by whether you've put in place a financial plan and a behavioral discipline that are likely to get you where you want to go."

Benjamin Graham

"I make no attempt to forecast the market—my efforts are devoted to finding undervalued securities."

Warren Buffett

"Though tempting, trying to time the market is a loser's game. $10,000 continuously invested in the market over the past 20 years grew to more than $48,000. If you missed just the best 30 days, your investment was reduced to $9,900.1"

Christopher Davis

The main reason to buy and hold stocks long-term is that long-term investments almost always outperform the market when investors try and time their investments. Emotional trading tends to hamstring investor returns.

Despite its popularity and presence in the news, the stock market is just one of many potential places to invest your money. Investing in stock is often risky, which draws attention to the huge gains and losses of some investors. If you manage the risks, you can take advantage of the stock market to secure your financial position and earn money.

Investment Gains

One of the primary benefits of investing in the stock market is the chance to grow your money. Over time, the stock market tends to rise in value, though the prices of individual stocks rise and fall daily. Investments in stable companies that are able to grow tend to make profits for investors. Likewise, investing in many different stocks will help build your wealth by leveraging growth in different sectors of the economy, resulting in a profit even if some of your individual stocks lose value.

Dividend Income

Some stocks provide income in the form of a dividend. While not all stocks offer dividends, those that do deliver annual payments to investors. These payments arrive even if the stock has lost value and represent income on top of any profits that come from eventually selling the stock. Dividend income can help fund a retirement or pay for even more investing as you grow your investment portfolio over time.

Diversification

For investors who put money into different types of investment products, a stock market investment has the benefit of providing diversification. Stock market investments change value independently of other types of investments, such as bonds and real estate. Holding stock can help you weather losses to other investment products. Stock also adds risk to a portfolio, as well as the potential for large, rapid gains, helping investors avoid risk-averse or overly conservative investment strategies.

Ownership

Buying shares of stock means taking on an ownership stake in the company you purchase stock in. This means that investing in the stock market also brings benefits that are part of being one of a business's owners. Shareholders vote on corporate board members and certain business decisions. They also receive annual reports to learn more about the company. Owning stock in the company you work for can be a way to express loyalty and tie your personal finances to the success of the business as a whole.

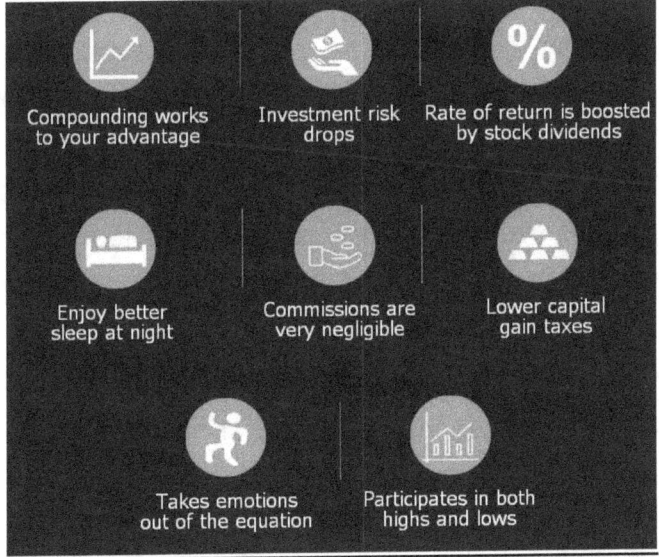

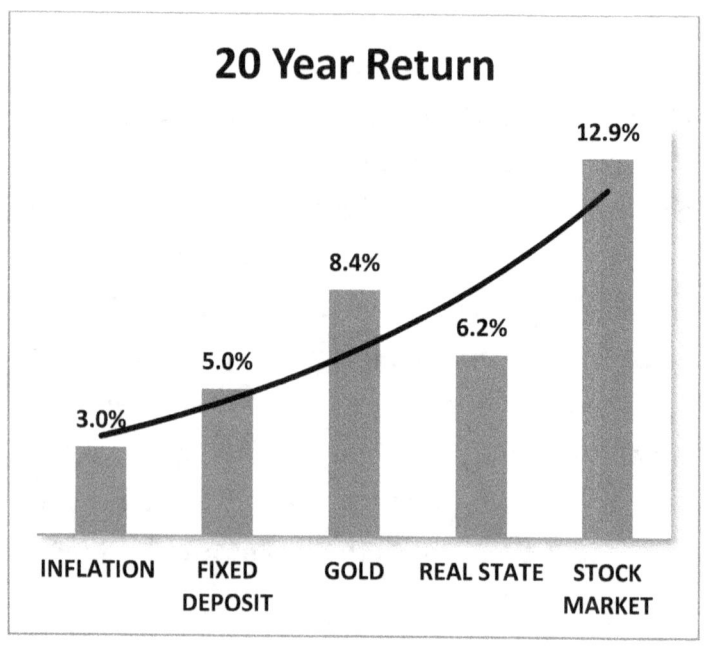

United State Different Assets Classes Return

In India Equity is the best asset class to help you create wealth. It beats inflation, and compounds at higher rates than your other products. In the last 30 years, the average return from equities (Sensex) has been ~14 per cent and inflation has been ~7 per cent.

March 13, 1986, the date a new company called Microsoft had its initial public offering (IPO). Cars that year retailed for around $10,000. But what if, instead of buying a car, you decided to purchase a block of shares in Microsoft? By 2020, that investment would be worth $13.7 million.

That is the reason why some people have much wealth and some people have sports car.

People do Mistake in Investment

Apple had three founders. Ronald Wayne was the third co-founder of Apple, along with Steve Wozniak and Steve Jobs. In 1976, he sold his 10% share of the company for $800. Today, his 10% would have been worth of $35 billion.

Some of the Greatest Investor in Stock market.

Benjamin Graham

Ben Graham excelled as an investment manager and financial educator. He authored, among other works, two investment classics of unparalleled importance. He is also universally recognized as the father of two fundamental investment disciplines—security analysis and value investing.

John Templeton

One of the past century's top contrarians, it is said about John Templeton that "he bought low during the Depression, sold high during the Internet boom, and made more than a few good calls in between." Templeton created some of the world's largest and most successful international investment funds. He sold his Templeton funds in 1992 to the Franklin Group. In 1999, Money magazine called him "arguably the greatest global stock picker of the century."

Peter Lynch

Peter Lynch managed the Fidelity Magellan Fund from 1977 to 1990, during which the fund's assets grew from $20 million to $14 billion. More importantly, Lynch reportedly beat the S&P 500 Index benchmark in 11 of those 13 years, achieving an annual average return of 29%.

Warren Buffett

Referred to as the "Oracle of Omaha," Warren Buffett is viewed as one of the most successful investors in history.

Following the principles set out by Benjamin Graham, he has amassed a multibillion dollar fortune mainly through buying stocks and companies through Berkshire Hathaway. Those who invested $10,000 in Berkshire Hathaway in 1965 are above the $50 million mark today.

John (Jack) Bogle

Bogle founded the Vanguard Group mutual fund company in 1974 and made it into one of the worlds largest and most respected fund sponsors. Bogle pioneered the no-load mutual fund and championed low-cost index investing for millions of investors.

Charlie Munger

Charles Thomas Munger is an American investor, businessman, former real estate attorney, and philanthropist. He is vice chairman of Berkshire Hathaway, the conglomerate controlled by Warren Buffett; Buffett has described Munger as his partner.

Philip Fisher

Philip Fisher is the father of investing in growth stocks. He started his own investment firm, Fisher & Company, in 1931, and managed it until his retirement in 1999 at the age of 91. Fisher achieved excellent returns for himself and his clients during his 70 year career.

The stock market is a vehicle to invest money, a proven method to achieve wealth while keeping up with inflation, comprised of publically held companies who offer goods and services that are used by the general public daily. Companies sell stocks to public investors in a free and open market environment on a daily basis, Stock investment means you are purchasing a share of the company, therefore the company's success determines the value of your investment.

Common stock is a term that is synonymous with investing; it is ownership in a public company. The stock owner is granted voting rights in addition the ability to receive dividends. Dividends is used often with the stock market, dividends are profit you receive when the company makes a profit. If the company does not make a profit, you will not receive a dividend reimbursement. Payments can be reinvested, which helps build wealth because you are increasing your portfolio. You can also so use this cash for whatever you like.

12

Time Value of Money

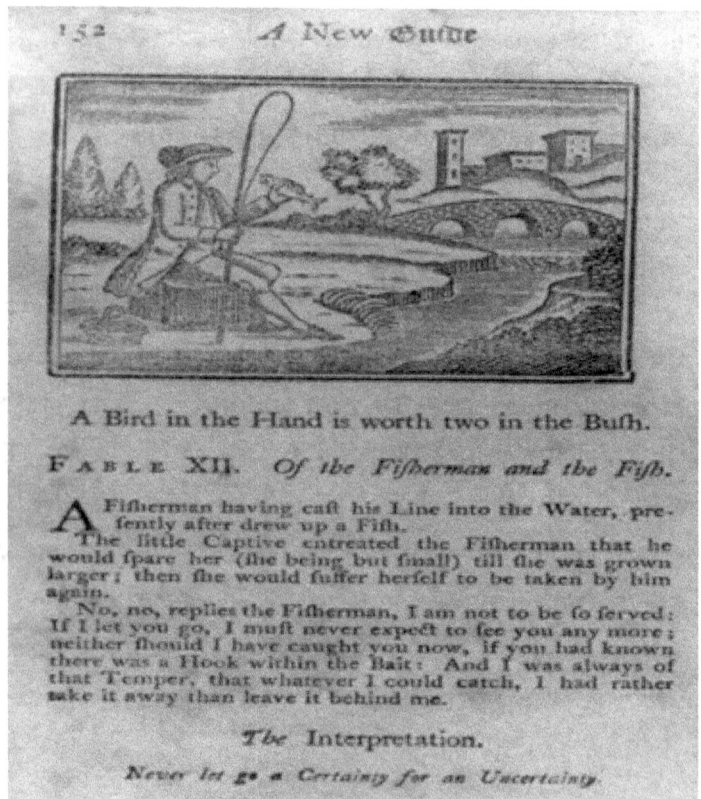

Proverbs (1670): 'A bird in the hand is worth two in the bush.

According to the Bible, *'A living dog is better than a dead lion.' (Ecclesiastes 9:4).* The earliest rendition of this proverb featuring birds instead of quadrupeds is to be found in Hugh Rhodes' Boke of Nature or School of Manners (1530), and may have been inspired by mediaeval falconry. Its current form first appears in John Ray's Hand-book of Proverbs (1670): 'A bird in the hand is worth two in the bush.' There is a similar proverb in the Czech language: *'A sparrow in the fist is better than a pigeon on the roof.'* The proverb and its variants suggest that, given the choice, the promise of less is preferable to the possibility of more.

Today money value more than something that is received later, the present value of cash received in future also less than the nominal value of the future amount.

Time value of money (TVM) is the idea that money that is available at the present time is worth more than the same amount in the future, due to its potential earning capacity. This core principle of finance holds that provided money can earn interest, any amount of money is worth more the sooner it is received. One of the most fundamental concepts in finance is that money has a time value attached to it. In simpler terms, it would be safe to say that a dollar was worth more yesterday than today and a dollar today is worth more than a dollar tomorrow.

Present value (PV) - This is your current starting amount. It is the money you have in your hand at the present time, your initial investment for your future.

Future value (FV) - This is your ending amount at a point in time in the future. It should be worth more than the present value, provided it is earning interest and growing over time.

The number of periods (N) - This is the timeline for your investment (or debts). It is usually measured in years, but it could be any scale of time such as quarterly, monthly, or even daily.

Interest rate (I) - This is the growth rate of your money over the lifetime of the investment. It is stated in a percentage value, such as 8% or .08.

The time value of money explains why interest is paid or earned: interest, whether it is on a bank deposit or debt, compensates the depositor or lender for the time value of money. The time value of money draws from the idea that rational investors prefer to receive money today rather than the same amount of money in the future because of money's potential to grow in value over a given period of time.

Time value of money is the difference between an amount of money in the present and that same amount of money in the future. Having money now is more valuable than having money later.

The present amount is called the present value, the future amount is called the future value, and the appropriate rate that relates the two amounts is called the discount rate.

Present Value = Future Value / (1 + Discount Rate)

Future Value = Present Value x (1 + Discount Rate)

Time Value of Money Examples

Now, let's look at time value of money examples. If you invest $100 (the present value) for 1 year at a 5% interest rate (the discount rate), then at the end of the year, you would have $105 (the future value). So, according to this example, $100 today is worth $105 a year from today.

$105 = $100 x 1.05

$100 = $105 / 1.05

Likewise, $100 a year from today, discounted back at 5%, is worth only $95.24 today.

$95.24 = $100 / 1.05

To calculate the time value of money for a period longer than one year, you simply raise the discount factor by the appropriate number of time periods. For example, to calculate the future value of $100 at 5% for 5 years:

$$\$127.63 = \$100 \times (1.05)^5$$

Value of Money Examples

Assume a sum of $10,000 is invested for one year at 10% interest. The future value of that money is:

$$FV = \$10,000 \times (1 + (10\% / 1))^{(1 \times 1)} = \$11,000$$

Money is worth more in the present than in the future because there's an opportunity cost to waiting for it. In addition to your loss of use if you don't get your hands on it right away, there's also inflation gradually eroding its value and purchasing power.

'A bird in hand is worth two in the bush' – this adage applies to financial transactions too. Say, someone borrowed a certain amount from you and it is due. Just as you are expecting the money to be credited to your account, you get a call from the borrower saying that he will pay you after 3 months. You are not happy about this.

Inflation increases prices over time, which means that each dollar you own today will buy more in the present time than it will in the future. This is why investing is so important.

Over time the stock market beats out inflation. So if you put the same amount of money in a savings account and investment account, the money invested would be worth far more than the money sitting in the savings account.

The Formula for Future Value

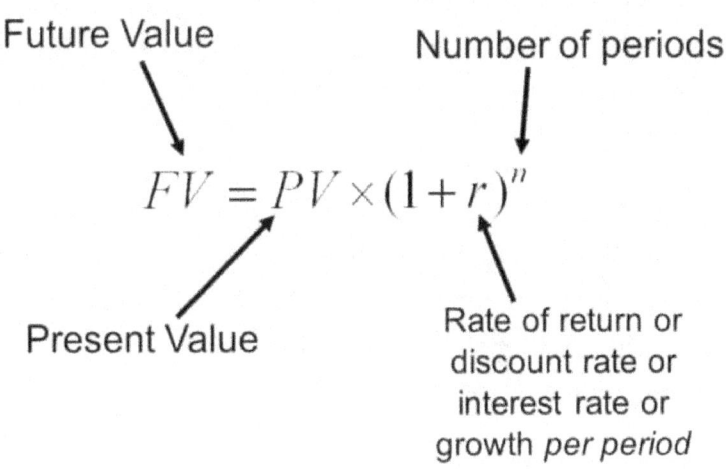

$$FV = PV \times (1+r)^n$$

- Future Value
- Number of periods
- Present Value
- Rate of return or discount rate or interest rate or growth *per period*

The car dealer gives you two choices:

1. Purchase the car for cash and receive a $2,000 instant cash rebate. This will make your out of pocket expense $16,000 today.

2. Or purchase the car for $18,000 with a zero percent interest 36-month loan. In this scenario, you would make monthly payments with a market interest rate of 4%.

Which is the cheaper option and how much will you save?

The correct answer is option 1: it will save you $935.38.

A mistake people make is comparing $16,000 to $18,000. If you choose Option A, you are paying out $16,000 now. If you choose Option B, you are paying monthly instalments of $500 for 36-months totalling $18, 000.

$FV = PV * (1 + i/n)n*$

Let us take an example of a sum of $100,000 today invested for two years at 12% rate of interest. Now let us calculate the future value of money if the compounding is done:

FV = $125,440

$PV = FV / (1 + i/n)n*t$

Let us take the example of a sum of $100,000 to be received after two years and the discounting rate is 10%. Now let us calculate the present value today if the compounding is done.

PV = $82,644

Stock Investing

"Other guys read Playboy, I read annual reports."
   Warren Buffett

13

Stock Investing

> *"I made my first investment at age eleven. I was wasting my life up until then."*
>
> — Warren Buffett

Stock market is a magic gateway to another world this world is full of privilege Street made of gold and image of man walking in tailor made suit and walking through a busy New York city street. Run across Financial news Trance tell us about the latest trend of the market you find money gross popping up with the book how to be millionaire .

A stock market, equity market or share market is the aggregation of buyers and transactions, not a physical facility of stocks also called shares , which represent ownership claims on businesses these may include securities listed on a public stock exchange,

The total market capitalization of equity backed securities worldwide rose from $2.5 trillion in 1980 to $68.65 trillion at the end of 2018. As of December 31, 2019, the total market capitalization of all stocks worldwide was approximately US$70.75 trillion.

In 12th-century France, the courretiers de changes were concerned with managing and regulating the debts of agricultural communities on behalf of the banks. Because these men also traded with debts, they could be called the first brokers. A common misbelieve is that, in late 13th-century Bruges, commodity traders gathered inside the house of a man called Van der Beurze, and in 1409 they became the "Brugse Beurse", institutionalizing what had been, until then, an informal meeting, but actually, the family Van der Beurze had a building in Antwerp where those gatherings occurred the Van der Beurze had Antwerp, as most of the merchants of that period, as their primary place for trading. The idea quickly spread around Flanders and neighbouring countries and "Beurzen" soon opened in Ghent and Rotterdam.

In the middle of the 13th century, Venetian bankers began to trade in government securities. In 1351 the Venetian government outlawed spreading rumours intended to lower the price of government funds. Bankers in Pisa, Verona, Genoa and Florence also began trading in government securities during the 14th century. This was only possible because these were independent city-states not ruled by a duke but a council of influential citizens. Italian companies were also the first to issue shares. Companies in England and the Low Countries followed in the 16th century. Around this time, a joint stock company--one whose stock is owned jointly by the shareholders--emerged and became important for colonization of what Europeans called the "New World".

The stock market is one of the most important ways for companies to raise money, along with debt markets which are generally more imposing but do not trade publicly. This allows businesses to be publicly traded, and raise additional financial capital for expansion by selling shares of ownership of the company in a public market. The liquidity that an exchange affords the investors enables their holders to quickly and easily sell securities. This is an attractive feature of investing in stocks, compared to other less liquid investments such as property and other immoveable assets.

As a result, a unique corporation was formed in 1600 called "Governor and Company of Merchants of London trading with the East Indies". This was the famous **East India Company** and it was the first company to use a limited liability formula.

Investors realized that putting all **their "eggs into one basket"** was not a smart way to approach investment in East Indies trading. Let's say that a ship returning from the East Indies had a 33% chance of being seized by pirates. Instead of investing in one voyage and risking the loss of all invested money, investors could purchase shares in multiple companies. Even if one ship was lost out of 3 or 4 invested companies, the investor would still make a profit.

The formula proved to be very successful. Within a decade, similar charters had been granted to other businesses throughout England, France, Belgium, and the Netherlands.

In 1602, the **Dutch East India Company** officially became the world's first publically traded company when it released shares of the company on the

Amsterdam Stock Exchange. Stocks and bonds were issued to investors and each investor was entitled to a fixed percentage of East India Company's profits.

Despite the ban on issuing shares, the London Stock Exchange was officially formed in 1801. Since companies were not allowed to issue shares until 1825, this was an extremely limited exchange. This prevented the London Stock Exchange from preventing a true global superpower.

That's why the creation of the New York Stock Exchange (NYSE) in 1817 was such an important moment in history.

The NYSE has traded stocks since its very first day. Contrary to what some may think, the NYSE wasn't the first stock exchange in the United States. The Philadelphia Stock Exchange holds that title. However, the NYSE soon became the most powerful stock exchange in the country due to the lack of any type of domestic competition and it's positioning at the centre of U.S. trade and economics in New York.

The London Stock Exchange was the main stock market for Europe, while the New York Stock Exchange was the main exchange for America and the world.

The list of the top 10 largest stock markets in the world by market capitalization:

- New York Stock Exchange
- NASDAQ
- Tokyo Stock Exchange
- London Stock Exchange Group
- Euronext
- Hong Kong Stock Exchange
- Shanghai Stock Exchange
- Toronto Stock Exchange
- Frankfurt Stock Exchange
- Australian Securities Exchange

The East India Company is widely recognized as the world's first publically traded company. There was one simple reason why the East India Company became the first publically traded company.

United East India Company

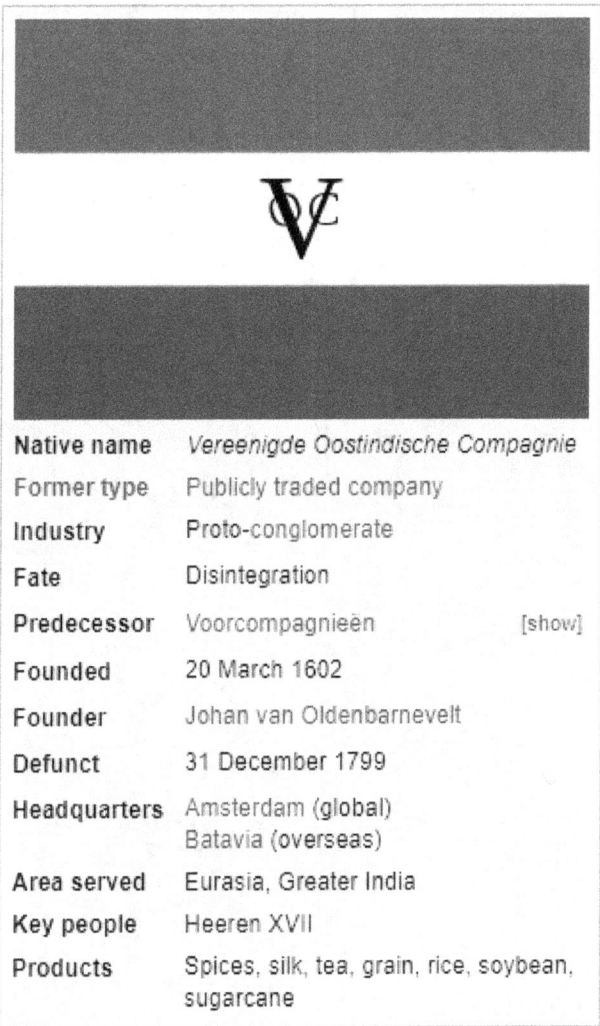

Native name	Vereenigde Oostindische Compagnie
Former type	Publicly traded company
Industry	Proto-conglomerate
Fate	Disintegration
Predecessor	Voorcompagnieën [show]
Founded	20 March 1602
Founder	Johan van Oldenbarnevelt
Defunct	31 December 1799
Headquarters	Amsterdam (global) Batavia (overseas)
Area served	Eurasia, Greater India
Key people	Heeren XVII
Products	Spices, silk, tea, grain, rice, soybean, sugarcane

The **Dutch East India Company**, officially the United East India Company (Dutch: Vereenigde Oostindische Compagnie; VOC) was a mega corporation founded by a government-directed amalgamation of several rival

Dutch trading companies in the early 17th century. It was established on 20 March 1602, as a chartered company to trade with Mughal India.

Replica of an East Indiaman of the Dutch East India Company/United East Indies Company (VOC). The Dutch East India Company was the first corporation to be listed on an official stock exchange. In 1611.

Crowd gathering on Wall Street (New York City) after the 1929 crash, one of the worst stock market crashes in history.

The New York Stock Exchange

Established in 1875, the Bombay Stock Exchange is Asia's oldest stock exchange.

The stock market is one of the most important components of a free-market economy, as it provides companies with access to capital in exchange for giving investors a part of ownership in the company. The share market makes possible to its investors to grow their small initial sums of money into large ones, and to become wealthy without taking the risk of starting a business as their own or making the sacrifices that often accompany a high-paying career.

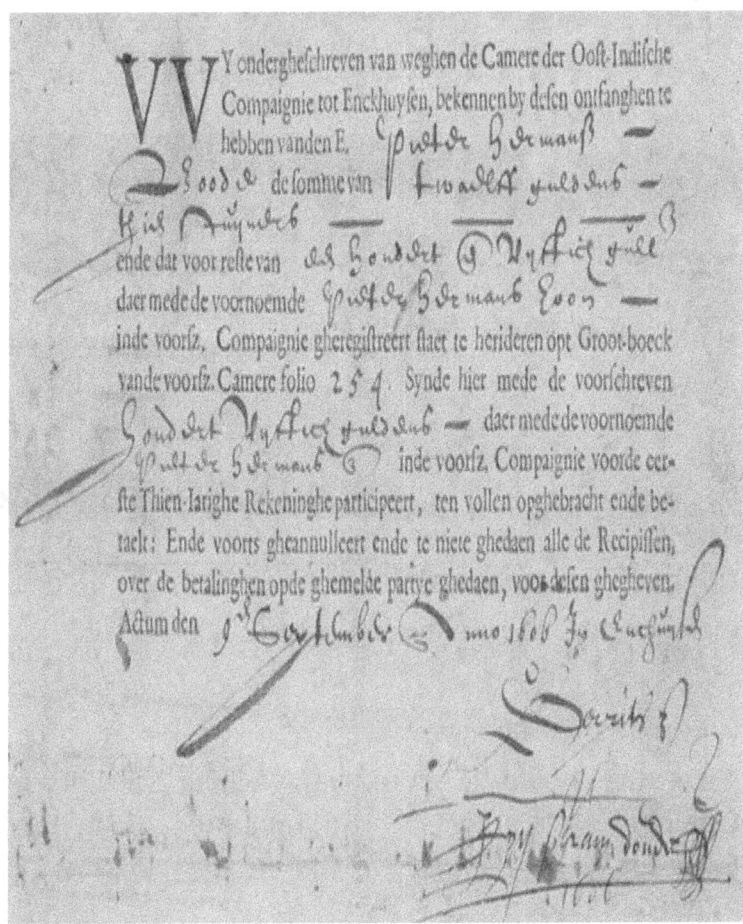

The first ever stock certificate issued, by the Dutch East India Company. The first Mega Company in the world

COMPANY ANALYSIS

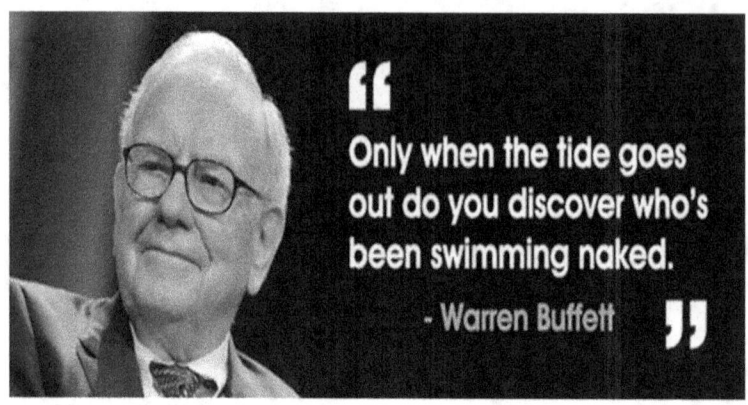

Do the necessary research, study, and analysis before making any investment decisions.

"Investing should be more like watching paint dry or watching grass grows. If you want excitement, take $800 and go to Las Vegas."
- **Paul Samuelson**

14
Financial Statement

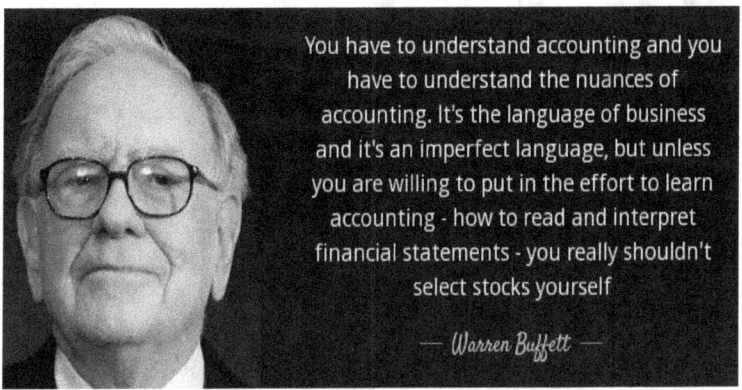

"Risk comes from not knowing what you're doing."

— *Warren Buffett*

"Rule No. 1 : Never lose money. Rule No. 2 : Never forget Rule No. 1."
— *Warren Buffett*

Using financial statement is a treasure map to discover the profit and cash flow and return the business give to their shareholders.

All financial statements are formal and legal statements aimed at reporting the entity's financial activities. They are prepared to provide true and fair information on changes in the company's performance, financial condition and financial condition. Major financial statements prepared for the company include income statement, balance sheet, and statement of changes in shareholders' equity and cash flow statement. As you can see from these statements, performance evaluations for that period are compared to other companies and past periods. The financial statements must give a true and fair view therefore auditors are responsible in detecting if there are risks of material misstatements caused by intentionally misstating or omitting items. Auditors must follow all ethical principles and should adhere to auditing standards in order to have an objective audit opinion.

Essentially, a company's financial statement shows readers the source of its income, the amounts that were spent to generate that income and the resulting profit or loss. The statement comprises three sub-statements, which are discussed below:

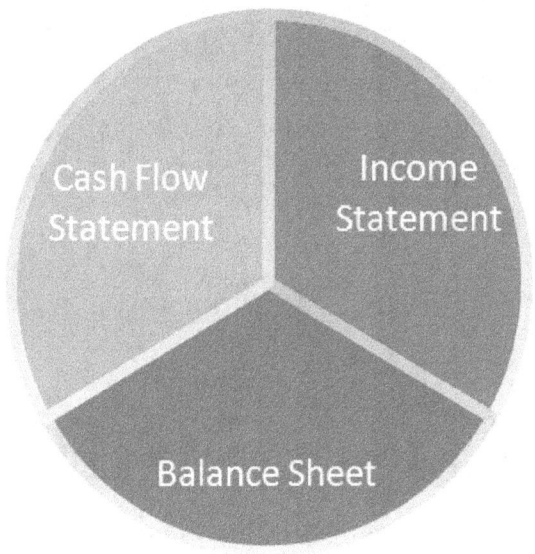

- **Balance sheet**
- **Income Statement**
- **Cash Flow Statement**

Balance Sheet

Assets can be anything from cash in a bank account to the factories used to build products. Some assets are physical entities and called tangible assets, while others are non-physical and called intangible assets.

Liabilities are debts or obligations taken on by a corporation; they can also be tangible and intangible. They include loans from banks, salaries of employees, taxes owed to the government and other obligations.

What's left after the liabilities are subtracted from the assets is shareholders' equity. Also known as "net worth," it tells shareholders how much would be left if the company had sold off all its assets and ceased operations on a specific date.

Income statement

He referred to it as a set of stairs:

At the top is the total (gross) revenue of the company.

Expenditures are deducted on one or more stairs.

The bottom step shows how much the corporation earned (or lost) after all expenses were deducted from all revenue.

Note that expenses include not only operating costs, but also depreciation and amortization. The latter refers to the periodic (usually annual) costs of an expenditure that is spread over multiple years. Interest expenses are also listed here, as is income earned from interest. And taxes are also shown in the income statement.

Finally, we see net income and the company's earnings per share, which are calculated by dividing net income by the number of outstanding shares. From this ratio, investors will learn how much they earned for each share they own.

Cash flow statement

Money comes in. Money goes out. You can find out in what proportions by studying the cash flow statement. While earnings per share in the income statement tells you whether a company made a profit, the cash flow statement "takes it a notch higher." That is, it can tell you whether the company was able to generate more cash than it paid out. It does that by providing data for three sets of activities.

The operating activities

This section of the cash flow statement, the company shows how much of its net income came from operations, i.e. the company's actual business. That is done by removing non-cash items from net income. One of the biggest non-cash items is often depreciation.

The investment activities

Section will show events such as the purchase of factories, equipment and property, as well as money put into investment securities. Consider a case in which the company buys a piece of property: cash will be exchanged for a piece of property that can be used to expand the company's business.

The Financing activities

Is the third type, It involves cash being received by the issuance of bonds or new shares, as well as money received from bank loans. On the other hand, cash flows out of a company when it repays a bank loan or buys back its own stock.

INCOME STATEMENT

The word accounting comes from the word accountability. If you are going to be rich, you need to be accountable for your money.

Robert Kiyosaki

15

Income Statement

Apple Inc Income Statement Sep-28-19	
$ Millions	
Revenues	2,60,174
Cost of goods sold	1,61,782
Gross profit	98,392
Gross Margin	*37.80%*
Operating Expenses	
Selling, General & administrative	18,245
Research & development	16,217
EBITA	63,930
EBITA Margin	*24.60%*
Other income/(expense), net	1,807
Income before provision for income taxes	65,737
EBIT Margin	*25.27%*
Income taxes	10,481
Tax rate	*15.90%*
Net income	55,256
Net margin	*21.24%*

Gross profit margin, operating profit margin, and net profit margin are the three main margin analysis measures that are used to analyze the income statement activities of a firm.

Each margin individually gives a very different perspective on the company's operational efficiency. Comprehensively the three margins taken together can provide insight into a firm's operational strengths and weaknesses

Gross Profit Margin

The gross profit margin seeks to identify how efficiently a company is producing its product. The calculation for gross profit margin is gross profit divided by total revenue. In general, it is better to have a higher gross profit margin number as it represents the total gross profit per dollar of revenue.

Operating Profit Margin or EBITA

Operating profit margin examines the effects of these costs. Operating profit is obtained by subtracting operating expenses from gross profit. The operating profit margin is then calculated by dividing the operating profit by total revenue.

Operating profit shows a company's ability to manage its indirect costs. Therefore, this section of the income statement shows how a company is investing in areas it expects will help to improve its brand and business growth through several channels.

Earnings before interest and taxes Margin

Earnings before interest and taxes (EBIT) is a company's net income before income tax expense and interest expense have been deducted. EBIT is used to analyze the performance of a company's core operations without tax expenses and the costs of the capital structure influencing profit

Net Profit Margin

Net profit margin is the third and final profit margin metric used in income statement analysis. It is calculated by analyzing the last section of the income statement and the net earnings of a company after accounting for all expenses.

16

Revenue

Apple Inc Income Statement Sep-28-19	
$ Millions	
Revenues	**2,60,174**
Cost of goods sold	1,61,782
Gross profit	98,392
Gross Margin	*37.80%*

The "Revenue" subheading begins the section of the statement that provides details about revenue earned during the period.

SALES REVENUE = SALES PRICE X NUMBER OF UNITS SOLD

Revenue, often referred to as sales, is the income received from normal business operations and other business activities. In accounting, revenue is the income that a business has from its normal business activities, usually from the sale of goods and services to customers. Revenue is also referred to as sales or turnover.

Also known as turnover, revenue is the total amount of money that a business has generated by selling of goods or services in over a defined period, such as a year. Often this figure refers to sales, although it can relate also to revenue from trading, financial speculation or any money-spinning activity. In other words, revenue is the income generated from business operations.

Example Apple Inc

	2019
iPhone [1]	$ 142,381
Mac [1]	25,740
iPad [1]	21,280
Wearables, Home and Accessories [1][2]	24,482
Services [3]	46,291
Total net sales [4]	$ 260,174

	2019
Net sales:	
U.S.	$ 102,266
China [1]	43,678
Other countries	114,230
Total net sales	$ 260,174

17

Cost of Goods Sold

Apple Inc Income Statement Sep-28-19

$ Millions	
Revenues	2,60,174
Cost of Goods sold	**1,61,782**
Gross Profit	98,392
Gross Margin	*37.80%*

This line lists the total wholesale cost of all of the goods you sold during the period.

Cost of goods sold, often abbreviated COGS, and is a managerial calculation that measures the direct costs incurred in producing products that were sold during a period. In other words, this is the amount of money the company spent on labor, materials, and overhead to manufacture or purchase products that were sold to customers during the year.

Cost of goods sold is the accumulated total of all costs used to create a product or service, which has been sold. These costs fall into the general sub-categories of direct labor, materials, and overhead. In a service business, the cost of goods sold is considered to be the labor, payroll taxes, and benefits of those people who generate billable hours (though the term may be changed to "cost of services"). In a retail or wholesale business, the cost of goods sold is likely to be merchandise that was bought from a manufacturer.

The cost of goods sold equation might seem a little strange at first, but it makes sense. Remember, we want to calculate the cost of the merchandise that was sold during the year, so we have to start with our beginning inventory.

We then add any new inventory that was purchased during the period. This gives us the total cost of all inventories, but we can't stop there. We only want to look at the cost of the inventory sold during the period. Thus, we have to subtract out the ending inventory to leave only the inventory that was sold.

COST OF GOODS SOLD = BEGINNING INVENTORY + PURCHASE - ENDING INVENTORY

Example Apple Inc

Cost of sales:	
Products	144,996
Services	16,786
Total cost of sales	161,782
Gross margin	98,392

18

Gross Profit

Apple Inc Income Statement Sep-28-19	
$ Millions	
Revenues	2,60,174
Cost of Goods sold	1,61,782
Gross Profit	**98,392**
Gross Margin	*37.80%*

Gross Profit is calculated by deducting the Cost of Goods Sold from Net Sales.

Gross profit margin is a profitability ratio that calculates the percentage of sales that exceed the cost of goods sold. In other words, it measures how efficiently a company uses its materials and labor to produce and sell products profitably. You can think of it as the amount of money from product sales left over after all of the direct costs associated with manufacturing the product have been paid. These direct costs are typically called cost of goods sold or COGS and usually consist of raw materials and direct labor.

GROSS PROFIT = TOTAL SALES - COST OF GOODS SOLD

Both the total sales and cost of goods sold are found on the income statement. Occasionally, COGS is broken down into smaller categories of costs like materials and labor. This equation looks at the pure dollar amount of GP for the company, but many times it's helpful to calculate the gross profit rate or margin as a percentage.

Gross profit is net sales minus the cost of goods sold. It reveals the amount that a business earns from the sale of its goods and services before the application of additional selling and administrative expenses. Gross profit is typically stated partway down the income statement, prior to a listing of selling, general, and administrative expenses.

Example Apple Inc

	2019
Gross margin:	
Products	$ 68,887
Services	29,505
Total gross margin	$ 98,392
Gross margin percentage:	
Products	32.2%
Services	63.7%
Total gross margin percentage	37.8%

19

Operating Expenses

Apple Inc Income Statement Sep-28-19

$ Millions	
Revenues	2,60,174
Cost of Goods sold	1,61,782
Gross Profit	98,392
Gross Margin	*37.80%*
Operating Expenses	
Selling, General & administrative	18,245
Research & development	16,217
EBITA	63,930
EBITA Margin	*24.60%*

The Operating Expenses subheading begins the section of the income statement that includes all of the expenses your company paid to operate during the period in question.

An operating expense is an expense a business incurs through its normal business operations. Often abbreviated as OPEX, operating expenses include rent, equipment, inventory costs, marketing, payroll, insurance, step costs, and funds allocated for research and development. One of the typical responsibilities that management must contend with is determining how to reduce operating expenses without significantly affecting a firm's ability to compete with its competitors.

Operating expenses are those expenditures that a business incurs to engage in activities not directly associated with the production of goods or services. These expenditures are the same as selling, general and administrative expenses.

Example Apple Inc

	2019
Research and development	$ 16,217
Percentage of total net sales	6%
Selling, general and administrative	$ 18,245
Percentage of total net sales	7%
Total operating expenses	$ 34,462
Percentage of total net sales	13%

20

Selling, General & Administrative Expenses

Apple Inc Income Statement Sep-28-19	
$ Millions	
Revenues	**2,60,174**
Cost of Goods sold	1,61,782
Gross Profit	98,392
Gross Margin	*37.80%*
Operating Expenses	
Selling, General & administrative	**18,245**
Research & development	16,217
EBITA	63,930
EBITA Margin	*24.60%*

Sales and Marketing – Beneath the Operating Expenses subheading, you will find a smaller subheading labeled "Sales and Marketing." In this section, you will find a list of all of the expenses your company incurred in relation to marketing. Examples include advertising, commissions and direct marketing. At the bottom of this section, you will find a total of these expenses.

General Administrative – This section of the document includes all of the administrative expenses paid during the period, including office supplies, utilities and more. At the end of this section, all general administrative expenses are totalled.

SG&A General & Administrative Expense (SG&A) refer to the expenses that a company makes, directly or indirectly, for the promotion, advertising, marketing and administration of the company as well as the compensation of the workforce, among others. Hence, SG & A include salaries, wages, and the associated taxes, utilities, marketing, advertising, promotion, sales, supplies, and insurance expenses.

The selling, general and administrative expense (SG&A) is comprised of all operating expenses of a business that are not included in the cost of goods sold. Management should maintain tight control over these costs, since they increase the breakeven point of a business. SG&A appears in the income statement, below the cost of goods sold.

Example Apple Inc

	2019
Research and development	$ 16,217
Percentage of total net sales	6%
Selling, general and administrative	$ 18,245
Percentage of total net sales	7%
Total operating expenses	$ 34,462
Percentage of total net sales	13%

From a management perspective, SG&A represents a large fixed cost that increases the breakeven point of a company, and therefore requires higher sales or higher product profits in order to turn a profit for the entire business. Consequently, it is especially important to maintain tight control over SG&A costs, which can be achieved through the continual review of discretionary costs, trend analysis, and comparisons of actual to budgeted costs. Zero-base budgeting can also be used to maintain control over the SG&A expense category.

21

Research & Development

Apple Inc Income Statement Sep-28-19	
$ Millions	
Revenues	2,60,174
Cost of Goods sold	1,61,782
Gross Profit	98,392
Gross Margin	*37.80%*
Operating Expenses	
Selling, General & administrative	18,245
Research & development	**16,217**
EBITA	63,930
EBITA Margin	*24.60%*

Research and development (R&D) is to any activity associated with creating new innovations in existing products, services, or procedures or the discovery of new innovations that lead to the creation new products. In other words, it's an ongoing process of investigation that looks forward to create new things.

Industries like pharmaceuticals, chemistry, military, and technology, R and D is a crucial department. If the companies in these industries aren't moving ahead, they are falling behind their competition. They must constantly be looking for ways to increase their products' effectiveness and come up with new ideas that will shape the market.

Example Apple Inc

	2019
Research and development	$ 16,217
Percentage of total net sales	6%
Selling, general and administrative	$ 18,245
Percentage of total net sales	7%
Total operating expenses	$ 34,462
Percentage of total net sales	13%

In industries like pharmaceuticals, chemistry, military, and technology, R and D is a crucial department. If the companies in these industries aren't moving ahead, they are falling behind their competition. They must constantly be looking for ways to increase their products' effectiveness and come up with new ideas that will shape the market.

Companies spend billions of dollars on R&D to produce the newest, most sought-after products. According to the professional services firm, PriceWaterhouseCoopers, the following ten companies spent the most on innovation and improvements in 2018.

- Amazon: $22.6 billion
- Alphabet, Inc.: $16.2 billion
- Volkswagen: $15.8 billion
- Samsung: $15.3 billion
- Intel: $13.1 billion
- Microsoft: $12.3 billion
- Apple: $11.6 billion
- Roche: $10.8 billion
- Johnson & Johnson: $10.6 billion
- Merck: $10.2 billion

22

Operating Income / EBITA

Apple Inc Income Statement Sep-28-19	
$ Millions	
Revenues	**2,60,174**
Cost of Goods sold	1,61,782
Gross Profit	98,392
Gross Margin	*37.80%*
Operating Expenses	
Selling, General & administrative	18,245
Research & development	16,217
EBITA	**63,930**
EBITA Margin	*24.60%*

Your Operating Income is the amount of income left over after all of your operating expenses are deducted from your gross profit.

The term "operating profit" refers to an accounting metric measuring the profits a company generates from its core business functions, where the deduction of interest and taxes is excluded from the calculation.

Next on the income statement is operating profit. Derived from gross profit, operating profit reflects the residual income that remains after accounting for all the costs of doing business. In addition to COGS, this includes fixed-cost expenses such as rent and insurance, variable expenses, such as shipping and freight, payroll and utilities, as well as amortization and depreciation of assets. All the expenses that are necessary to keep the business running must be included.

Operating Profit = Gross Profit - Operating Expenses

23

Other Income / Expenses, Net

Apple Inc Income Statement Sep-28-19	
$ Millions	
Revenues	2,60,174
Cost of Goods sold	1,61,782
Gross Profit	98,392
Gross Margin	*37.80%*
Operating Expenses	
Selling, General & administrative	18,245
Research & development	16,217
EBITA	63,930
EBITA Margin	*24.60%*
Other income/(expense), net	**1,807**
Income before provision for income taxes	65,737
EBIT Margin	*25.27%*

Income and expenses generated or lost from sources not directly related to a business' core operations.

Examples include income produced from the sale of assets or expenses accrued from lender frees due to overdrawing.

The entire disclosure for other income or other expense items (both operating and non operating). Sources of non operating income or non operating expense that may be disclosed, include amounts earned from dividends, interest on securities, profits (losses) on securities, net and miscellaneous other income or income deductions.

Example Apple Inc

	2019
Interest and dividend income	$ 4,961
Interest expense	(3,576)
Other income/(expense), net	422
Total other income/(expense), net	$ 1,807

24

EBIT

Apple Inc Income Statement Sep-28-19

$ Millions	
Revenues	2,60,174
Cost of Goods sold	1,61,782
Gross Profit	98,392
Gross Margin	*37.80%*
Operating Expenses	
Selling, General & administrative	18,245
Research & development	16,217
EBITA	63,930
EBITA Margin	*24.60%*
Other income/(expense), net	1,807
Income before provision for income taxes	**65,737**
EBIT Margin	*25.27%*

The value on this line is calculated by adding your Operating Income and Non operating Income and then subtracting your Non operating Expenses.

Investors and creditors use EBIT because it allows them to look at how successful the core operations of the company are without having to worry about the tax ramifications or the cost of the capital structure. They can simply look at whether the business activities and ideas behind them actually work in the real world

EBIT = Total Revenues - COGS - Operating Expenses

25

Provision for Income Taxes

Apple Inc Income Statement Sep-28-19	
$ Millions	
Revenues	2,60,174
Cost of Goods sold	1,61,782
Gross Profit	98,392
Gross Margin	*37.80%*
Operating Expenses	
Selling, General & administrative	18,245
Research & development	16,217
EBITA	63,930
EBITA Margin	*24.60%*
Other income/(expense), net	1,807
Income before provision for income taxes	65,737
EBIT Margin	*25.27%*
Provision for income taxes	**10,481**
Tax rate	**15.90%**

As stated, the income tax amount has not actually been paid it is an estimate or an account that has been created to cover the amount a company expects to pay in taxes.

This section includes all of the taxes your business paid during the period, including prepaid income tax and payroll taxes.

Example Apple Inc

	2019
Computed expected tax	$ 13,805
State taxes, net of federal effect	423
Impacts of the Act	—
Earnings of foreign subsidiaries	(2,625)
Research and development credit, net	(548)
Excess tax benefits from equity awards	(639)
Other	65
Provision for income taxes	$ 10,481
Effective tax rate	15.9%

26

Net Income

Apple Inc Income Statement Sep-28-19	
$ Millions	
Revenues	2,60,174
Cost of Goods sold	1,61,782
Gross Profit	98,392
Gross Margin	*37.80%*
Operating Expenses	
Selling, General & administrative	18,245
Research & development	16,217
EBITA	63,930
EBITA Margin	*24.60%*
Other income/(expense), net	1,807
Income before provision for income taxes	65,737
EBIT Margin	*25.27%*
Provision for income taxes	10,481
Tax rate	*15.90%*
Net income	**55,256**
Net margin	*21.24%*

The final line on your income statement is your total net income. It is calculated by subtracting your total Taxes from Income before Taxes. If your expenses for the period exceeded your income, this value will be negative, representing an overall loss.

Net income after taxes (NIAT) is a financial term used to describe a company's profit after all taxes have been paid. Net income after taxes is an accounting term and is most often found in a company's quarterly and annual financial reports. Net income after taxes represent the profit or earnings after all expense have been deducted from revenue. Net income after taxes calculation can be shown as both a total dollar amount and a per-share calculation.

Net income represents the amount of money remaining after all operating expenses, interest, taxes and preferred stock dividends (but not common stock dividends) have been deducted from a company's total revenue. Net income is also referred to as the bottom line, net profit or net earnings.

Net Income = Total Revenue - Total Expenses

27

Earnings Per share

Apple Inc

	2019
Numerator:	
Net income	$ 55,256
Denominator:	
Weighted-average basic shares outstanding	4,617,834
Effect of dilutive securities	31,079
Weighted-average diluted shares	4,648,913
Basic earnings per share	$ 11.97
Diluted earnings per share	$ 11.89

Earnings per share (EPS) is calculated as a company's profit divided by the outstanding shares of its common stock. The resulting number serves as an indicator of a company's profitability.

A higher EPS indicates more value because investors will pay more for a company with higher profits. EPS indicates how much money a company makes for each share of its stock and is a widely used metric for corporate profits.

Earnings per share or EPS are an important financial measure, which indicates the profitability of a company. It is calculated by dividing the company's net income with its total number of outstanding shares. It is a tool that market participants use frequently to gauge the profitability of a company before buying its shares.

EPS is a financial ratio, which divides net earnings available to common shareholders by the average outstanding shares over a certain period of time. The EPS formula indicates a company's ability to produce net profits for common shareholders. This guide breaks down the Earnings per Share formula in detail.

$$EPS = \frac{\text{Net Income - Preferred Dividends}}{\text{Weighted Average Shares Outstanding}}$$

BALANCE SHEET

Accounting is the language of business.
Warren Buffett

28

Balance Sheet

Apple Inc CONSOLIDATED BALANCE SHEETS Sep-28-19 $ Millions	
ASSETS:	
Current assets:	
Cash and equivalents	48,844
Marketable securities	51,713
Accounts receivable, net	22,926
Inventories	4,106
Vendor non-trade receivables	22,878
Other current assets	12,352
Total current assets	1,62,819
Non-current assets:	
Marketable securities	1,05,341
Property, plant, and equipment, net	37,378
Other non-current assets	32,978
Total non-current assets	1,75,697
Total assets	3,38,516
LIABILITIES AND SHAREHOLDERS' EQUITY	
Current liabilities:	
Accounts payable	46,236
Other current liabilities	37,720
Deferred revenue	5,522
Commercial paper	5,980
Term debt	10,260
Total current liabilities	1,05,718
Non-current liabilities:	
Long-term debt	91,807
Other non-current liabilities	50,503
Total non-current liabilities	1,42,310
Total liabilities	2,48,028
Total shareholders' equity	90,488
Total liabilities and shareholders' equity	3,38,516

A balance sheet is a financial statement that reports a company's assets, liabilities and shareholders' equity at a specific point in time, and provides a basis for computing rates of return and evaluating its capital structure. It is a financial statement that provides a snapshot of what a company owns and owes, as well as the amount invested by shareholders.

Assets = Liabilities + Shareholders' Equity

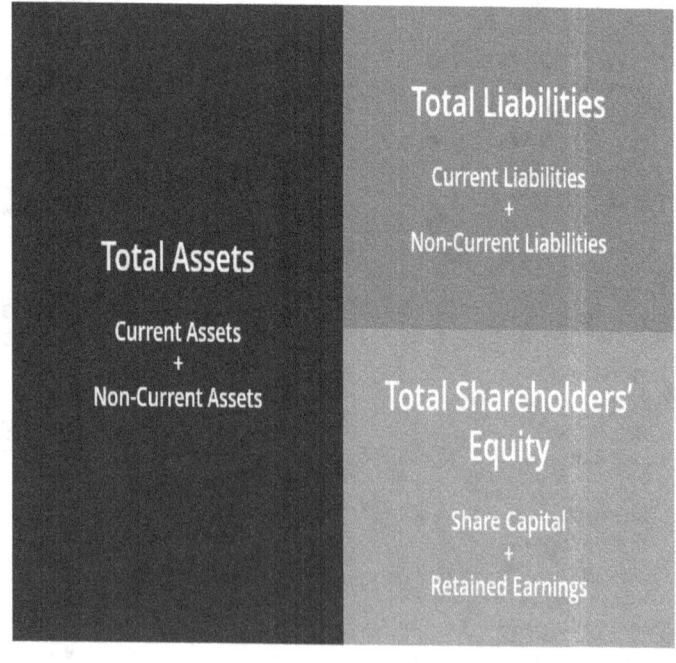

A Simple Balance Sheet

Assets

Within the assets segment, accounts are listed from top to bottom in order of their liquidity – that is, the ease with which they can be converted into cash. They are divided into current assets, which can be converted to cash in one year or less; and non-current or long-term assets, which cannot.

One can classify assets into two major asset classes: tangible assets and intangible assets. Tangible assets contain various subclasses, including current assets and fixed assets. Current assets include inventory, while fixed assets include such items as buildings and equipment. Intangible assets are nonphysical resources and rights that have a value to the firm because they give the firm some kind of advantage in the marketplace. Examples of intangible assets include goodwill, copyrights, trademarks, patents and computer programs, and financial assets, including such items as accounts receivable, bonds and stocks.

Liabilities

Liabilities are the money that a company owes to outside parties, from bills it has to pay to suppliers to interest on bonds it has issued to creditors to rent, utilities and salaries. Current liabilities are those that are due within one year and are listed in order of their due date. Long-term liabilities are due at any point after one year.

Liabilities are reported on a balance sheet and are usually divided into two categories:

Current liabilities — these liabilities are reasonably expected to be liquidated within a year. They usually include payables such as wages, accounts, taxes, and accounts payable, unearned revenue when adjusting entries, portions of long-term bonds to be paid this year, short-term obligations (e.g. from purchase of equipment).

Long-term liabilities — these liabilities are reasonably expected not to be liquidated within a year. They usually include issued long-term bonds, notes payables, long-term leases, pension obligations, and long-term product warranties.

Shareholders' Equity

Shareholders' equity is the money attributable to a business' owners, meaning its shareholders. It is also known as "net assets," since it is equivalent to the total assets of a company minus its liabilities, that is, the debt it owes to non-shareholders. Shareholders equity is the amount that shows how the company has been financed with the help of common shares and preferred shares. Shareholders equity is also called Share Capital, Stockholder's Equity or Net worth.

By knowing how to analyze a company's financial information, you can determine:

- How much debt the business has relative to its equity.
- How quickly customers are paying their bills
- Whether short-term cash is declining or increasing.
- The percentage of assets that are tangible (e.g., factories, plants, and machinery) and how much comes from accounting transactions.
- Whether products are being returned at higher-than-average historical rates.
- How many days it takes, on average, to sell the inventory the business keeps on hand.
- Whether the research and development budget is producing good results.
- Whether the interest coverage ratio on the bonds is declining.
- The average interest rate a company is paying on its debt.
- Where profits are being spent or reinvested.

29

Cash & Cash Equivalents

Apple Inc CONSOLIDATED BALANCE SHEETS Sep-28-19 $ Millions	
ASSETS:	
Current assets:	
Cash and equivalents	48,844
Marketable securities	51,713
Accounts receivable, net	22,926
Inventories	4,106
Vendor non-trade receivables	22,878
Other current assets	12,352
Total current assets	**1,62,819**

Cash and cash equivalents refers to the line item on the balance sheet that reports the value of a company's assets that are cash or can be converted into cash immediately. Cash equivalents include bank accounts and marketable securities, which are debt securities with maturities of less than 90 days. However, oftentimes cash equivalents do not include equity or stock holdings because they can fluctuate in value.

Cash and cash equivalents help companies with their working capital needs since these liquid assets are used to pay off current liabilities, which are short-term debts and bills.

Cash equivalents are investments that can readily be converted into cash. The investment must be short term, usually with maximum investment duration of three months or less. If an investment matures in more than three months, it should be classified in the account named "other investments." Cash equivalents should be highly liquid and easily sold on the market. The buyers of these investments should be easily accessible.

The most liquid current assets found on a business's balance sheet. Cash equivalents are short-term commitments "with temporarily idle cash and easily convertible into known cash amount one of the company's crucial health indicators is its ability to generate cash and cash equivalents. So, a company with relatively high net assets and significantly less cash and cash equivalents can mostly be considered an indication of non-liquidity. For investors and company's cash and cash equivalents are generally counted to be "low risk and low return" investments and sometimes analysts can estimate company's ability to pay its bills in a short period of time by comparing CCE and current liabilities. Nevertheless, this can happen only if there are receivables that can be converted into cash immediately.

Example Apple Inc

	Cash and Cash Equivalents
Cash	$ 12,204
Level 1 [1]:	
Money market funds	15,897
Subtotal	15,897
Level 2 [2]:	
U.S. Treasury securities	6,165
U.S. agency securities	6,489
Non-U.S. government securities	749
Certificates of deposit and time deposits	2,024
Commercial paper	5,193
Corporate debt securities	123
Municipal securities	—
Mortgage- and asset-backed securities	—
Subtotal	20,743
Total [3]	$ 48,844

30

Marketable Securities

Apple Inc CONSOLIDATED BALANCE SHEETS Sep-28-19 $ Millions	
ASSETS:	
Current assets:	
Cash and equivalents	48,844
Marketable securities	51,713
Accounts receivable, net	22,926
Inventories	4,106
Vendor non-trade receivables	22,878
Other current assets	12,352
Total current assets	**1,62,819**

If these securities and/or debt are anticipated to be converted into cash within one year, they are listed at their current market value, in the Current Assets section of the balance sheet. If they are not trading securities, they are listed as Non Current Assets. Held to maturity and available for sale, securities can either be listed as long term or short term, depending on the maturity dates of the securities and the intention of management regarding conversion of these securities

Marketable securities are assets that can be liquidated to cash quickly. These short-term liquid securities can be bought or sold on a public stock exchange or a public bond exchange. These securities tend to mature in a year or less and can be either debt or equity. Marketable securities include common stock, Treasury bills, and money market instruments, among others.

Businesses typically hold cash in their reserves to prepare them for situations in which they may need to act swiftly, such as taking advantage of an acquisition opportunity that comes up or making contingent payments. However, instead of holding on to all the cash in its coffers which presents no opportunity to earn interest, a business will invest a portion of the cash in short-term liquid securities. This way, instead of having cash sit idly, the company can earn returns on it. If a sudden need for cash emerges, the company can easily liquidate these securities. Examples of short-term investment products are a group of assets categorized as marketable securities.

Example Apple Inc

	Short-Term Marketable Securities
Cash	$ —
Level 1 [1]:	
Money market funds	—
Subtotal	—
Level 2 [2]:	
U.S. Treasury securities	9,817
U.S. agency securities	2,249
Non-U.S. government securiti	3,168
Certificates of deposit and tim deposits	1,922
Commercial paper	7,240
Corporate debt securities	26,127
Municipal securities	68
Mortgage- and asset-backed securities	1,122
Subtotal	51,713
Total [3]	$ 51,713

31

Accounts Receivable, Net

Apple Inc CONSOLIDATED BALANCE SHEETS Sep-28-19 $ Millions	
ASSETS:	
Current assets:	
Cash and equivalents	48,844
Marketable securities	51,713
Accounts receivable, net	22,926
Inventories	4,106
Vendor non-trade receivables	22,878
Other current assets	12,352
Total current assets	**1,62,819**

Net receivables are the total money owed to a company by its customers minus the money owed that will likely never be paid. Net receivables are often expressed as a percentage, and a higher percentage indicates a business has a greater ability to collect from its customers.

A company can improve its cash collections by tightening control over credit issued to customers, maintaining efficient collection procedures, and performing collection procedures promptly.

Net receivables are the amount of money owed by customers that a business expects them to actually pay. This information is used to measure the credit and collection effectiveness of an organization, and can also be included in the cash forecast to measure projected cash inflows. A large difference between gross receivables and net receivables indicates a significant problem with either the credit granting or collection activities of a business.

Investors compare net receivables to accounts receivable to find the net receivable percentage. This percentage is important as it shows how effectively the company can collect from its borrowers. The closer a company's net receivables percentage is to 100%, the more effective they are at collecting from customers, and the more financially stable the company is.

Example Apple Inc

Accounts Receivable

Trade Receivables

The Company has considerable trade receivables outstanding with its third-party cellular network carriers, wholesalers, retailers, resellers, small and mid-sized businesses and education, enterprise and government customers. The Company generally does not require collateral from its customers; however, the Company will require collateral or third-party credit support in certain instances to limit credit risk. In addition, when possible, the Company attempts to limit credit risk on trade receivables with credit insurance for certain customers or by requiring third-party financing, loans or leases to support credit exposure. These credit-financing arrangements are directly between the third-party financing company and the end customer. As such, the Company generally does not assume any recourse or credit risk sharing related to any of these arrangements.

As of September 28, 2019, the Company had no customers that individually represented 10% or more of total trade receivables. As of September 29, 2018, the Company had one customer that represented 10% or more of total trade receivables, which accounted for 10%. The Company's cellular network carriers accounted for 51% and 59% of total trade receivables as of September 28, 2019 and September 29, 2018, respectively.

32

Inventories

Apple Inc CONSOLIDATED BALANCE SHEETS Sep-28-19 $ Millions	
ASSETS:	
Current assets:	
Cash and equivalents	48,844
Marketable securities	51,713
Accounts receivable, net	22,926
Inventories	4,106
Vendor non-trade receivables	22,878
Other current assets	12,352
Total current assets	**1,62,819**

Inventory is the term for the goods available for sale and raw materials used to produce goods available for sale. Inventory represents one of the most important assets of a business because the turnover of inventory represents one of the primary sources of revenue generation and subsequent earnings for the company's shareholders.

Inventory can be valued in three ways. The first-in, first-out (FIFO) method says that the cost of goods sold is based on the cost of the earliest purchased materials, while the carrying cost of remaining inventory is based on the cost of the latest purchased materials. The last-in, first-out (LIFO) method states that the cost of goods sold is valued using the cost of the latest purchased materials, while the value of the remaining inventory is based on the earliest purchased materials. The weighted average method requires valuing both inventory and the cost of goods sold based on the average cost of all materials bought during the period. The goods and materials that a business holds for the ultimate goal of resale.

Inventories refer to the closing stock of goods a company has at the end of a specific period (usually a financial year). It includes raw materials, finished goods and work-in-progress. The company must value their inventories using the guidelines of the accounting standards.

Example Apple Inc

Inventories

Inventories are measured using the first-in, first-out method.

33

Vendor Non –Trade Receivable

Apple Inc CONSOLIDATED BALANCE SHEETS Sep-28-19 $ Millions	
ASSETS:	
Current assets:	
Cash and equivalents	48,844
Marketable securities	51,713
Accounts receivable, net	22,926
Inventories	4,106
Vendor non-trade receivables	22,878
Other current assets	12,352
Total current assets	1,62,819

Non trade receivables are amounts due for payment to an entity other than its normal customer invoices for merchandise shipped or services performed. Examples of non trade receivables are amounts owed to a company by its employees for loans or wage advances, tax refunds owed to it by taxing authorities, or insurance claims owed to it by an insurance company.

"The Company has non-trade receivables from certain of its manufacturing vendors resulting from the sale of raw material components to these manufacturing vendors who manufacture sub-assemblies or assemble final products for the Company. The Company purchases these raw material components directly from suppliers."

Example Apple Inc

Vendor Non-Trade Receivables

The Company has non-trade receivables from certain of its manufacturing vendors resulting from the sale of components to these vendors who manufacture sub-assemblies or assemble final products for the Company. The Company purchases these components directly from suppliers. As of September 28, 2019, the Company had two vendors that individually represented 10% or more of total vendor non-trade receivables, which accounted for 59% and 14%. As of September 29, 2018, the Company had two vendors that individually represented 10% or more of total vendor non-trade receivables, which accounted for 62% and 12%.

34

Other Current Assets

Apple Inc CONSOLIDATED BALANCE SHEETS Sep-28-19 $ Millions	
ASSETS:	
Current assets:	
Cash and equivalents	48,844
Marketable securities	51,713
Accounts receivable, net	22,926
Inventories	4,106
Vendor non-trade receivables	22,878
Other current assets	12,352
Total current assets	1,62,819

Other current assets (OCA) is a category of things of value that a company owns, benefits from, or uses to generate income that can be converted into cash within one business cycle. They are referred to as "other" because they are uncommon or insignificant, unlike typical current asset items such as cash, securities, accounts receivable, inventory, and prepaid expenses.

Current assets, on the other hand, are all the assets of a company that are expected to be conveniently sold, consumed, utilized, or exhausted through standard business operations. They can easily be liquidated for cash, usually within one year, and are considered when calculating a firm's ability to pay short-term liabilities. Examples of current assets include cash and cash equivalents (CCE), marketable securities, accounts receivable, inventory, and prepaid expenses.

35

Total Current Assets

Apple Inc CONSOLIDATED BALANCE SHEETS Sep-28-19 $ Millions	
ASSETS:	
Current assets:	
Cash and equivalents	48,844
Marketable securities	51,713
Accounts receivable, net	22,926
Inventories	4,106
Vendor non-trade receivables	22,878
Other current assets	12,352
Total current assets	**1,62,819**

Total current assets are the aggregate amount of all cash, receivables, prepaid expenses, and inventory on an organization's balance sheet. These assets are classified as current assets if there is an expectation that they will be converted into cash within one year. The total amount of current assets is frequently compared to total current liabilities, to see if there are sufficient assets available to pay for the obligations of a business.

Current assets include cash, cash equivalents, accounts receivable, stock inventory, marketable securities, pre-paid liabilities, and other liquid assets. In a few jurisdictions, the term is also known as current accounts. Current assets are defined as all assets that can be expected to be converted to cash or equivalents within one year and are also known as short-term assets

Classification of assets is based on two groups, current assets and non-current or long-term assets. If a property is convertible to cash easily within one calendar year or less, it is known as a Current asset. Resources that are of value and are liquid are all assets. Current assets are used to pay current liabilities. Examples of current assets include cash in hand, cash at bank, accounts receivable and inventory. Current assets are used to fund the day-to-day running of the business. On a balance sheet, under the assets column, the first item listed is current assets.

36

Marketable securities

Non-current assets:	
Marketable securities	1,05,341
Property, plant, and equipment, net	37,378
Other non-current assets	32,978
Total non-current assets	**1,75,697**
Total assets	**3,38,516**

Long term Marketable securities are liquid financial instruments that can be quickly converted into cash at a reasonable price. The liquidity of marketable securities comes from the fact that the maturities tend convert after one year, and that the rates at which they can be bought or sold have little effect on prices.

Marketable securities are defined as any unrestricted financial instrument that can be bought or sold on a public stock exchange or a public bond exchange. Therefore, marketable securities are classified as either marketable equity security or marketable debt security. Other requirements of marketable securities include having a strong secondary market that can facilitate quick buy and sell transactions, and having a secondary market that provides accurate price quotes for investors. The return on these types of securities is low, due to the fact that marketable securities are highly liquid and are considered safe investments.

Example Apple Inc

	Long-Term Marketable Securities
Cash	$ —
Level 1 [1]:	
Money market funds	—
Subtotal	—
Level 2 [2]:	
U.S. Treasury securities	14,282
U.S. agency securities	1,027
Non-U.S. government securities	16,191
Certificates of deposit and time deposits	95
Commercial paper	—
Corporate debt securities	59,797
Municipal securities	897
Mortgage- and asset-backed securities	13,052
Subtotal	105,341
Total [3]	$ 105,341

37

Property, Plant & Equipment, Net

Non-current assets:	
Marketable securities	1,05,341
Property, plant, and equipment, net	**37,378**
Other non-current assets	32,978
Total non-current assets	1,75,697
Total assets	**3,38,516**

Net PP&E is short for Net Property Plant and Equipment. Property Plant and Equipment is the value of all buildings, land, furniture, and other physical capital that a business has purchased to run its business. The term "Net" means that it is "Net" of accumulated depreciation expenses.

Property, plant, and equipment (PP&E) are long-term assets vital to business operations and not easily converted into cash. Property, plant, and equipment are tangible assets, meaning they are physical in nature or can be touched. The total value of PP&E can range from very low to extremely high compared to total assets. It is important to note when calculating equity.

Property, plant, and equipment basically include any of a company's long-term, fixed assets. PP&E assets are tangible, identifiable, and expected to generate an economic return for the company for more than one year or one operating cycle (whichever is longer). The account can include machinery, equipment, vehicles, buildings, land, office equipment, and furnishings, among other things. Note that, of all these asset classes, land is one of the only assets that does not typically depreciate over time.

If a company produces machinery (for sale), that machinery does not classify as property, plant, and equipment. The machinery used to produce the machinery for sales is PP&E, but the machinery manufactured for sale is classified as inventory. The same goes for real estate companies that hold buildings and land under their assets. Their office buildings and land are PP&E, but the houses they sell are inventory.

Example Apple Inc

Property, Plant and Equipment, Net

	2019
Land and buildings	$ 17,085
Machinery, equipment and internal-use software	69,797
Leasehold improvements	9,075
Gross property, plant and equipment	95,957
Accumulated depreciation and amortization	(58,579)
Total property, plant and equipment, net	$ 37,378

	2019
Long-lived assets:	
U.S.	$ 24,711
China [1]	9,064
Other countries	3,603
Total long-lived assets	$ 37,378

38

Other Non-Current Assets

Non-current assets:	
Marketable securities	1,05,341
Property, plant, and equipment, net	37,378
Other non-current assets	32,978
Total non-current assets	1,75,697
Total assets	**3,38,516**

Noncurrent assets are a company's long-term investments for which the full value will not be realized within the accounting year. Examples of noncurrent assets include investments in other companies, intellectual property (e.g. patents), and property, plant and equipment. Noncurrent assets appear on a company's balance sheet.

Other noncurrent assets include the cash surrender value of life insurance. A bond sinking fund established for the future repayment of debt is classified as a noncurrent asset. Some deferred income taxes, goodwill, trademarks, and unamortized bond issue costs are noncurrent assets as well.

The assets which are not Current Assets or Fixed Assets or Investment Asset shall be classified under the head 'Other Non-Current Assets'. The 'Dead Inventories' which are separated from items of current assets, 'Receivables' outstanding beyond one year(which is also called deferred receivables), Advances made to staff, partners, directors, Advances made for acquisition of fixed assets, Margin for non-fund based facilities' intercorporate investments, security deposits, and any other miscellaneous assets shall be classified as other non-current assets.

39

Total non-current assets

Non-current assets:	
Marketable securities	1,05,341
Property, plant, and equipment, net	37,378
Other non-current assets	32,978
Total non-current assets	1,75,697
Total assets	3,38,516

Total non – current assets include Noncurrent assets are reported under the following balance sheet headings:

- Investments (long-term)
- Property, plant and equipment
- Intangible assets
- Other assets

40

Total assets

Apple Inc CONSOLIDATED BALANCE SHEETS Sep-28-19 $ Millions	
ASSETS:	
Current assets:	
Cash and equivalents	48,844
Marketable securities	51,713
Accounts receivable, net	22,926
Inventories	4,106
Vendor non-trade receivables	22,878
Other current assets	12,352
Total current assets	1,62,819
Non-current assets:	
Marketable securities	1,05,341
Property, plant, and equipment, net	37,378
Other non-current assets	32,978
Total non-current assets	1,75,697
Total assets	**3,38,516**

Total assets refer to the total amount of assets owned by a person or entity. Assets are items of economic value, which are expended over time to yield a benefit for the owner. If the owner is a business, these assets are usually recorded in the accounting records and appear in the balance sheet of the business. Typical categories in which these assets may be found include:

- Cash
- Marketable securities
- Accounts receivable
- Prepaid expenses
- Inventory
- Fixed assets
- Intangible assets
- Goodwill
- Other assets

Assets are also classified on the balance sheet as either current assets or long-term assets. A current asset, such as an account receivable or marketable security, is expected to be liquidated within one year. A long-term asset, such as a fixed asset, is expected to be liquidated in more than one year.

41

Accounts Payable

LIABILITIES AND SHAREHOLDERS' EQUITY	
Current liabilities:	
Accounts payable	46,236
Other current liabilities	37,720
Deferred revenue	5,522
Commercial paper	5,980
Term debt	10,260
Total current liabilities	**1,05,718**

Accounts payable (AP) is an account within the general ledger that represents a company's obligation to pay off a short-term debt to its creditors or suppliers. Another common usage of "AP" refers to the business department or division that is responsible for making payments owed by the company to suppliers and other creditors.

Accounts payable (AP) is an important figure in a company's balance sheet. If AP increases over a prior period, that means the company is buying more goods or services on credit, rather than paying cash. If a company's AP decreases, it means the company is paying on its prior period debts at a faster rate than it is purchasing new items on credit. Accounts payable management is critical in managing a business's cash flow.

Accounts payable (AP) is money owed by a business to its suppliers shown as a liability on a company's balance sheet In households, accounts payable are ordinarily bills from the electric company, telephone company, cable television or satellite dish service, newspaper subscription, and other such regular services. Householders usually track and pay on a monthly basis by hand using cheques, credit cards or internet banking. In a business, there is usually a much broader range of services in the AP file, and accountants or bookkeepers usually use accounting software to track the flow of money into this liability account when they receive invoices and out of it when they make payments. Increasingly, large firms are using specialized Accounts Payable automation solutions (commonly called ePayables) to automate the paper and manual elements of processing an organization's invoices. Accounts payable and its management is a critical business process through which an entity manages its payable obligations effectively. Accounts payable is the amount owed by an entity to its vendors/suppliers for the goods and services received.

42

Other Current Liabilities

LIABILITIES AND SHAREHOLDERS' EQUITY	
Current liabilities:	
Accounts payable	46,236
Other current liabilities	37,720
Deferred revenue	5,522
Commercial paper	5,980
Term debt	10,260
Total current liabilities	1,05,718

Other current liabilities, in financial accounting, are categories of short-term debt that are lumped together on the balance sheet. The term "current liabilities" refers to items of short-term debt that a firm must pay within 12 months. To that, companies add the word "other" to describe those current liabilities that are not significant enough to identify separately on their own lines in financial statements, so they are grouped together as "other current liabilities." Other current liabilities are the opposite of other current assets.

Depending on the company and its industry, you will see many kinds of items listed under other current liabilities. Usually, you can find explanations of these "other" liabilities somewhere in the company's annual report or Form 10-K; they also may be detailed in the footnotes to the financial statements.

Accounts payable is typically one of the largest current liability accounts on a company's financial statements, and it represents unpaid supplier invoices. Companies try to match payment dates so that their accounts receivables are collected before the accounts payables are due to suppliers.

Other current liabilities are a line item in the balance sheet, which aggregates several current liability accounts that are too minor to report separately. The contents of this line item may be explained in more detail in the accompanying footnotes.

43

Deferred Revenue

LIABILITIES AND SHAREHOLDERS' EQUITY	
Current liabilities:	
Accounts payable	46,236
Other current liabilities	37,720
Deferred revenue	5,522
Commercial paper	5,980
Term debt	10,260
Total current liabilities	1,05,718

Deferred revenue refers to payments received in advance for services which have not yet been performed or goods which have not yet been delivered. These revenues are classified on the company's balance sheet as a liability and not as an asset. Deferred revenue is important in accurate reporting of assets and liabilities on a company's balance sheet. It protects against treating unearned income as an asset, and guards against overvaluing the company's net worth. While cash is usually the safest asset a company owns, not all cash is equal: Cash that is classified as deferred revenues is at risk until the work is performed. Deferred revenues are important to a company because they finance operations without encumbering other company assets or drawing on a credit line.

Deferred revenue is most common among companies selling subscription-based products or services that require prepayments. Deferred revenue is a liability because it reflects revenue that has not been earned and represents products or services that are owed to a customer. As the product or service is delivered over time, it is recognized proportionally as revenue on the income statement.

Example Apple Inc

Deferred Revenue

As of September 28, 2019 and September 29, 2018, the Company had total deferred revenue of $8.1 billion and $8.8 billion, respectively. As of September 28, 2019, the Company expects 68% of total deferred revenue to be realized in less than a year, 25% within one-to-two years, 6% within two-to-three years and 1% in greater than three years.

44

Commercial Paper

LIABILITIES AND SHAREHOLDERS' EQUITY	
Current liabilities:	
Accounts payable	46,236
Other current liabilities	37,720
Deferred revenue	5,522
Commercial paper	5,980
Term debt	10,260
Total current liabilities	**1,05,718**

Commercial paper is a commonly used type of unsecured, short-term debt instrument issued by corporations, typically used for the financing of payroll, accounts payable and inventories, and meeting other short-term liabilities. Maturities on commercial paper typically last several days, and rarely range longer than 270 days. Commercial paper is usually issued at a discount from face value and reflects prevailing market interest rates.

Commercial paper is not usually backed by any form of collateral, making it a form of unsecured debt. As a result, only firms with high-quality debt ratings will easily find buyers without having to offer a substantial discount (higher cost) for the debt issue. Because commercial paper is issued by large institutions, the denominations of the commercial paper offerings are substantial, usually $100,000 or more. Other corporations, financial institutions, wealthy individuals, and money market funds are usually buyers of commercial paper.

Commercial paper, in the global financial market, is an unsecured promissory note with a fixed maturity of rarely more than 270 days.

Example Apple Inc

The Company believes its existing balances of cash, cash equivalents and marketable securities, along with commercial paper and other short-term liquidity arrangements, will be sufficient to satisfy its working capital needs, capital asset purchases, dividends,
Share repurchases, debt repayments and other liquidity requirements associated with its existing operations over the next 12 months.

Debt -The Company issues unsecured short-term promissory notes ("Commercial Paper") pursuant to a commercial paper program. The Company uses the net proceeds from the commercial paper program for general corporate purposes, including dividends and share repurchases. As of September 28, 2019, the

Company had $6.0 billion of Commercial Paper outstanding, with a weighted-average interest rate of 2.24% and maturities generally less than nine months.

45

Term Debts

LIABILITIES AND SHAREHOLDERS' EQUITY	
Current liabilities:	
Accounts payable	46,236
Other current liabilities	37,720
Deferred revenue	5,522
Commercial paper	5,980
Term debt	10,260
Total current liabilities	**1,05,718**

Short-term debt, also called current liabilities, is a firm's financial obligations that are expected to be paid off within a year. It is listed under the current liabilities portion of the total liabilities section of a company's balance sheet. Operating debt arises from the primary activities that are required to run a business, such as accounts payable, and is expected to be resolved within 12 months, or within the current operating cycle, of its accrual. This is known as short-term debt and is usually made up of short-term bank loans taken out, or commercial paper issued, by a company.

The value of the short-term debt account is very important when determining a company's performance. Simply put, the higher the debt to equity ratio, the greater the concern about company liquidity. If the account is larger than the company's cash and cash equivalents, this suggests that the company may be in poor financial health and does not have enough cash to pay off its impending obligations.

Example Apple Inc

Term Debt

As of September 28, 2019, the Company had outstanding floating- and fixed-rate notes with varying maturities for an aggregate principal amount of $101.7 billion (collectively the "Notes"). The Notes are senior unsecured obligations and interest is payable in arrears. The following table provides a summary of the Company's term debt as of September 28, 2019 and September 29, 2018.

	Maturities (calendar year)	Amount (in millions)	2019 Effective Interest Rate
2013–2018 debt issuances:			
Floating-rate notes	2020 – 2022	$ 4,250	2.25% – 3.28%
Fixed-rate 0.350% – 4.650% notes	2019 – 2047	90,429	0.28% – 4.78%
2019 debt issuance:			
Fixed-rate 1.700% – 2.950% notes	2022 – 2049	7,000	1.71% – 2.99%
Total term debt		101,679	
Unamortized premium/(discount) and issuance costs, net		(224)	
Hedge accounting fair value adjustments		612	
Less: Current portion of term debt		(10,260)	
Total non-current portion of term debt		$ 91,807	

46

Total Current Liabilities

LIABILITIES AND SHAREHOLDERS' EQUITY	
Current liabilities:	
Accounts payable	46,236
Other current liabilities	37,720
Deferred revenue	5,522
Commercial paper	5,980
Term debt	10,260
Total current liabilities	**1,05,718**

Also called Current Liabilities and listed on the Balance Sheet, the Total Current Liabilities are the claims to the company's assets that are due within one year or the cycle of operations. Total Current Liabilities usually make up several line items, such as Accounts Payable, Notes Payable, Current Maturities, and Accrued Liabilities.

Current liabilities are typically settled using current assets, which are assets that are used up within one year.

47

Long –Term Debts

Non-current liabilities:	
Long-term debt	91,807
Other non-current liabilities	50,503
Total non-current liabilities	1,42,310
Total liabilities	**2,48,028**
Total shareholders' equity	90,488
Total liabilities and shareholders' equity	**3,38,516**

Long-term debt is debt that matures in more than one year. Long-term debt can be viewed from two perspectives: financial statement reporting by the issuer and financial investing. In financial statement reporting, companies must record long-term debt issuance and all of its associated payment obligations on its financial statements. On the flip side, investing in long-term debt includes putting money into debt investments with maturities of more than one year.

Long-term debt issuance has a few advantages over short-term debt. Interest from all types of debt obligations, short and long, are considered a business expense that can be deducted before paying taxes.

Longer-term debt usually requires a slightly higher interest rate than shorter term debt. However, a company has a longer amount of time to repay the principal with interest.

Long Term Debt (LTD) is any amount of outstanding debt a company holds that has a maturity of 12 months or longer. It is classified as a non-current liability on the company's balance sheet. The time to maturity for LTD can range anywhere from 12 months to 30+ years and the types of debt can include bonds, mortgages, bank loans, debentures, etc

Example Apple Inc

Term Debt
As of September 28, 2019, the Company had outstanding floating- and fixed-rate notes with varying maturities for an aggregate principal amount of $101.7 billion (collectively the "Notes"). The Notes are senior unsecured obligations and interest is payable in arrears. The following table provides a summary of the Company's term debt as of September 28, 2019 and September 29, 2018:

	Maturities (calendar year)	2019 Amount (in millions)	Effective Interest Rate
2013–2018 debt issuances:			
Floating-rate notes	2020 – 2022	$ 4,250	2.25% – 3.28%
Fixed-rate 0.350% – 4.650% notes	2019 – 2047	90,429	0.28% – 4.78%
2019 debt issuance:			
Fixed-rate 1.700% – 2.950% notes	2022 – 2049	7,000	1.71% – 2.99%
Total term debt		101,679	
Unamortized premium/(discount) and issuance costs, net		(224)	
Hedge accounting fair value adjustments		612	
Less: Current portion of term debt		(10,260)	
Total non-current portion of term debt		$ 91,807	

48

Other Non-Current Liabilities

Non-current liabilities:	
Long-term debt	91,807
Other non-current liabilities	50,503
Total non-current liabilities	1,42,310
Total liabilities	2,48,028
Total shareholders' equity	90,488
Total liabilities and shareholders' equity	3,38,516

Noncurrent liabilities, also called long-term liabilities or long-term debts, are long-term financial obligations listed on a company's balance sheet. These liabilities have obligations that become due beyond twelve months in the future, as opposed to current liabilities which are short-term debts with maturity dates within the following twelve month period.

Analysts also use coverage ratios to assess a company's financial health, including the cash flow-to-debt and the interest coverage ratio. The cash flow-to-debt ratio determines how long it would take a company to repay its debt if it devoted all of its cash flow to debt repayment. The interest coverage ratio, which is calculated by dividing a company's earnings before interest and taxes (EBIT) by its debt interest payments for the same period, gauges whether enough income is being generated to cover interest payments. To assess short-term liquidity risk, analysts look at liquidity ratios like the current ratio, the quick ratio, and the acid test ratio.

Noncurrent liabilities are those obligations not due for settlement within one year. These liabilities are separately classified in an entity's balance sheet, away from current liabilities. Examples of noncurrent liabilities are:

- Long-term portion of debt payable.

- Long-term portion of bonds payable.

Example Apple Inc

Other Non-Current Liabilities

	2019
Long-term taxes payable	$ 29,545
Other non-current liabilities	20,958
Total other non-current liabilities	$ 50,503

49

Total Non-Current Liabilities

Non-current liabilities:	
Long-term debt	91,807
Other non-current liabilities	50,503
Total non-current liabilities	**1,42,310**
Total liabilities	**2,48,028**
Total shareholders' equity	90,488
Total liabilities and shareholders' equity	**3,38,516**

Noncurrent liabilities include debentures, long-term loans, bonds payable, deferred tax liabilities, long-term lease obligations, and pension benefit obligations. The portion of a bond liability that will not be paid within the upcoming year is classified as a noncurrent liability. Warranties covering more than a one-year period are also recorded as noncurrent liabilities. Other examples include deferred compensation, deferred revenue, and certain health care liabilities.

Mortgages, car payments, or other loans for machinery, equipment, or land are all long-term debts, except for the payments to be made in the subsequent twelve months which are classified as the current portion of long-term debt. Debt that is due within twelve months may also be reported as a noncurrent liability if there is intent to refinance this debt with a financial arrangement in the process to restructure the obligation to a noncurrent nature.

50

Total Shareholders' Equity

Non-current liabilities:	
Long-term debt	91,807
Other non-current liabilities	50,503
Total non-current liabilities	1,42,310
Total liabilities	**2,48,028**
Total shareholders' equity	90,488
Total liabilities and shareholders' equity	**3,38,516**

Firm's total assets minus its total liabilities. Equivalently, it is share capital plus retained earnings minus treasury shares. Shareholders' equity represents the amount by which a company is financed through common and preferred shares.

Shareholders' Equity = Total Assets - Total Liabilities

It is important to understand that shareholders equity does not represent surplus cash or cash left over after the payment of dividends. Rather, shareholders equity demonstrates what a company did with its profits and capital -- it is the amount the owners (the shareholders) have invested in the business since its inception. These reinvestments are either asset purchases or liability reductions

Shareholder equity represents the amount of money that would be returned to shareholders if all of the assets were liquidated and all of the company's debt was paid off. Retained earnings are part of shareholder equity and is the percentage of net earnings that were not paid to shareholders as dividends. Think of retained earnings as savings since it represents a cumulative total of profits that have been saved and put aside or retained for future use.

Example Apple Inc

Shareholders' equity:	
Common stock and additional paid-in capital, $0.00001 par value: 12,600,000 shares authorized; 4,443,236 and 4,754,986 shares issued and outstanding, respectively	45,174
Retained earnings	45,898
Accumulated other comprehensive income/(loss)	(584)
Total shareholders' equity	90,488
Total liabilities and shareholders' equity	$ 338,516

CASH FLOW STATEMENT

"Never take your eyes off the cash flow because it's the lifeblood of business."

——Richard Branson

51

Cash Flow Statement

In financial accounting, a cash flow statement, also known as statement of cash flows or funds flow statement is a financial statement that shows how changes in balance sheet accounts and income affect cash and cash equivalents, and breaks the analysis down to operating, investing, and financing activities. The primary purpose of a statement of cash flows is to provide relevant information about the cash receipts and cash payments of an enterprise during a period.

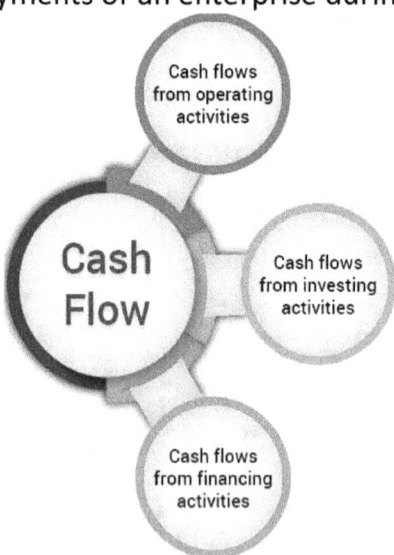

Components of cash flow statement:

Operating activities:

Operating activities are the functions of a business directly related to providing its goods and/or services to the market. These are the company's core business activities, such as manufacturing, distributing, marketing, and selling a product or service. Operating activities will generally provide the majority of a company's cash flow and largely determine whether it is profitable. Some common operating activities include cash receipts from goods sold, payments to employees, taxes, and payments to suppliers. These activities can be found on a company's financial statements and in particular the income statement and cash flow statement.

Operating activities are distinguished from investing or financing activities, which are functions of a company not directly related to the provision of goods and services. Instead, financing and investing activities help the company function optimally over the longer term. This means that the issuance of stock or bonds by a company are not counted as operating activities.

Investing activities:

Cash flow from investing activities is one of the sections on the cash flow statement that reports how much cash has been generated or spent from various investment-related activities in a specific period. Investing activities include purchases of physical assets, investments in securities, or the sale of securities or assets.

Negative cash flow is often indicative of a company's poor performance. However, negative cash flow from investing activities might be due to significant amounts of cash being invested in the long-term health of the company, such as research and development.

Financing activities:

Financing activities include borrowing and repaying money, issuing stock (equity) and paying dividends. It relates to the long-term debt and stockholders' equity. They include borrowing cash from creditors and repayment of such loans and the sale of capital stock and the payment of dividends and return of capital to equity investors. For example, if you borrow funds to purchase equipment or pay off a loan, the cash flow statement will enable you to determine how much cash was either generated or used as a result of those transactions.

Example Apple Inc

Apple Inc CONSOLIDATED STATEMENTS OF CASH FLOWS	
$ Millions	2019
Operating activities:	
Net income	55,256
Adjustments to reconcile net income to cash generated by operating activities:	
Depreciation and amortization	12,547
Share-based compensation expense	6,068
Deferred income tax expense/(benefit)	-340
Other	-652
Changes in operating assets and liabilities:	
Accounts receivable, net	245
Inventories	-289
Vendor non-trade receivables	2,931
Other current and non-current assets	873
Accounts payable	-1,923
Deferred revenue	-625
Other current and non-current liabilities	-4,700
Cash generated by operating activities	**69,391**
Investing activities:	
Purchases of marketable securities	-39,630
Proceeds from maturities of marketable securities	40,102
Proceeds from sales of marketable securities	56,988
Payments for acquisition of property, plant and equipment	-10,495
Payments made in connection with business acquisitions, net	-624
Purchases of non-marketable securities	-1,001
Proceeds from non-marketable securities	1,634
Other	-1,078
Cash generated by/(used in) investing activities	**45,896**
Financing activities:	
Proceeds from issuance of common stock	781
Payments for taxes related to net share settlement of equity awards	-2,817
Payments for dividends and dividend equivalents	-14,119
Repurchases of common stock	-66,897
Proceeds from issuance of term debt, net	6,963
Repayments of term debt	-8,805
Proceeds from/(Repayments of) commercial paper, net	-5,977
Other	-105
Cash used in financing activities	**-90,976**
Increase/(Decrease) in cash, cash equivalents and restricted cash	24,311
Cash, cash equivalents and restricted cash, ending balances	**50,224**
Supplemental cash flow disclosure:	15,263
Cash paid for income taxes, net	3,423
Cash paid for interest	

52

Operating Activities

Apple Inc CONSOLIDATED STATEMENTS OF CASH FLOWS	
$ Millions	2019
Operating activities:	
Net income	55,256
Adjustments to reconcile net income to cash generated by operating activities:	
Depreciation and amortization	12,547
Share-based compensation expense	6,068
Deferred income tax expense/(benefit)	-340
Other	-652
Changes in operating assets and liabilities:	
Accounts receivable, net	245
Inventories	-289
Vendor non-trade receivables	2,931
Other current and non-current assets	873
Accounts payable	-1,923
Deferred revenue	-625
Other current and non-current liabilities	-4,700
Cash generated by operating activities	69,391

Operating activities are the daily activities of a company involved in producing and selling its product, generating revenues, as well as general administrative and maintenance activities. The operating income shown on a company's financial statements is the operating profit remaining after deducting operating expenses from operating revenues. There is typically an operating activities section of a company's statement of cash flows that shows inflows and outflows of cash resulting from a company's key operating activities.

In the event of ambiguity, operating activities can readily be identified by classification in financial statements. Many companies report operating income or income from operations as a specific line on the income statement. Operating income is calculated by subtracting the cost of sales (COGS), research and development (R&D) expenses selling and marketing expenses, general and administrative expenses, and depreciation and amortization expenses.

Operating income excludes interest income or expenses. For example, an apparel stores operating activities might include the following:

- Operating activities are the daily activities of a company involved in producing and selling its product, generating revenues, as well as general administrative and maintenance activities.
- Key operating activities for a company include manufacturing, sales, advertising, and marketing activities.
- Cash flows from operations are an important metric used by financial analysts and investors.

53

Investing Activities

Investing activities:	
Purchases of marketable securities	-39,630
Proceeds from maturities of marketable securities	40,102
Proceeds from sales of marketable securities	56,988
Payments for acquisition of property, plant and equipment	-10,495
Payments made in connection with business acquisitions, net	-624
Purchases of non-marketable securities	-1,001
Proceeds from non-marketable securities	1,634
Other	-1,078
Cash generated by/(used in) investing activities	**45,896**

Investing activities are one of the main categories of net cash activities that businesses report on the cash flow statement. Investing activities in accounting refers to the purchase and sale of long-term assets and other business investments, within a specific reporting period. A business's reported investing activities give insights into the total investment gains and losses it experienced during a defined period. Investing activities are a crucial component of a company's cash flow statement, which reports the cash that's earned and spent over a certain period of time.

Fixed assets are property and equipment that a business owns and uses to help generate revenue. Fixed assets are less liquid than current assets and are not meant to be converted into cash within a year. Some examples of fixed assets include:

- Buildings and property
- Vehicles
- Machinery
- Computers
- Software
- Furniture

54

Financing Activities

Financing activities:	
Proceeds from issuance of common stock	781
Payments for taxes related to net share settlement of equity awards	-2,817
Payments for dividends and dividend equivalents	-14,119
Repurchases of common stock	-66,897
Proceeds from issuance of term debt, net	6,963
Repayments of term debt	-8,805
Proceeds from/(Repayments of) commercial paper, net	-5,977
Other	-105
Cash used in financing activities	**-90,976**

Financing activities are transactions involving long-term liabilities, owner's equity and changes to short-term borrowings. These activities involve the flow of cash and cash equivalents between the company and its sources of finance i.e. the investors and creditors for non-trading liabilities such as long-term loans, bonds payable etc.

The cash flow from financing activities is the funds that the business took in or paid to finance its activities. It's one of the three sections on a company's statement of cash flows, the other two being operating and investing activities.

Some examples of cash flows from financing activities are:

- Issuing bonds (positive cash flow).
- Sale of treasury stock (positive cash flow).
- Loan from a financial institution (positive cash flow).
- Repayment of existing loans (negative cash flow).
- Cash from new stock issued (positive cash flow).
- Payment of cash dividend to stockholders (negative cash flow).
- Purchase of treasury stock (negative cash flow).
- Repurchase of existing stock (negative cash flow).
- Redemption of bonds (negative cash flow).

55

Free Cash Flow

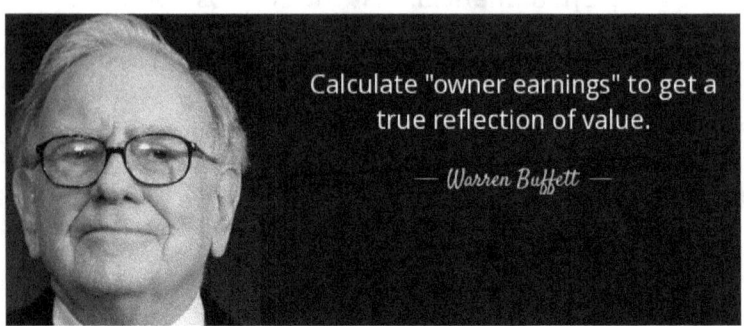

Calculate "owner earnings" to get a true reflection of value.

— *Warren Buffett* —

Free cash flow is the cash a company produces through its operations, less the cost of expenditures on assets. In other words, free cash flow (FCF) is the cash left over after a company pays for its operating expenses and capital expenditures, also known as CAPEX.

Free cash flow is an important measurement since it shows how efficient a company is at generating cash. Investors use free cash flow to measure whether a company might have enough cash, after funding operations and capital expenditures, to pay investors through dividends and share buybacks.

FCF=Operating Cash Flow – Capital Expenditures

Example Apple Inc

Apple Inc.

CONSOLIDATED STATEMENTS OF CASH FLOWS

(In millions)

	September 28, 2019
Cash, cash equivalents and restricted cash, beginning balances	$ 25,913
Operating activities:	
Net income	55,256
Adjustments to reconcile net income to cash generated by operating activities:	
Depreciation and amortization	12,547
Share-based compensation expense	6,068
Deferred income tax expense/(benefit)	(340)
Other	(652)
Changes in operating assets and liabilities:	
Accounts receivable, net	245
Inventories	(289)
Vendor non-trade receivables	2,931
Other current and non-current assets	873
Accounts payable	(1,923)
Deferred revenue	(625)
Other current and non-current liabilities	(4,700)
Cash generated by operating activities	69,391
Investing activities:	
Payments for acquisition of property, plant and equipment	(10,495)
Free Cash Flow	58,896

Valuation

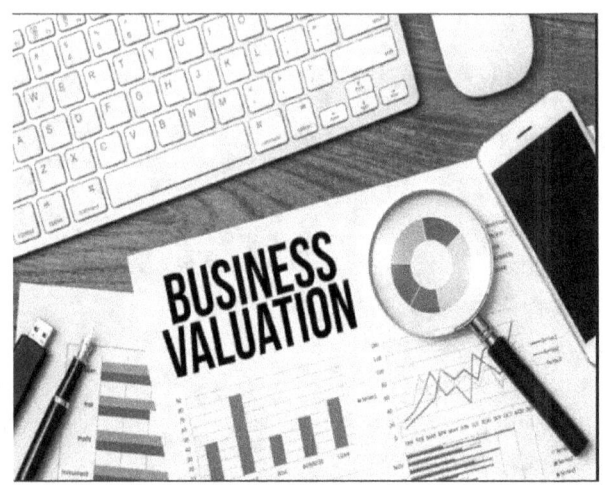

"Forecasts may tell you a great deal about the forecaster; they tell you nothing about the future."

— Warren Buffett

56

Discounted Cash Flow

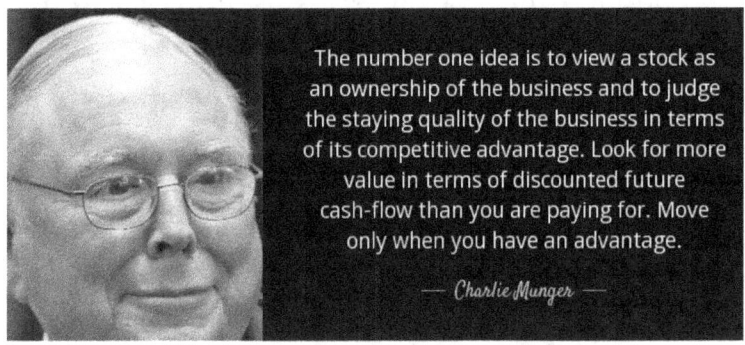

Warren Buffett thoughts on Intrinsic Value

Intrinsic value is an all-important concept that offers the only logical approach to evaluating the relative attractiveness of investments and businesses. Intrinsic value can be defined simply: It is the discounted value of the cash that can be taken out of a business during its remaining life.

The calculation of intrinsic value, though, is not so simple. As our definition suggests, intrinsic value is an estimate rather than a precise figure, and it is additionally an estimate that must be changed if interest rates move or forecasts of future cash flows are revised. Two people looking at the same set of facts, moreover – and this would apply even to Charlie and me – will almost inevitably come up with at least slightly different intrinsic value figures. That is one reason we never give you our estimates of intrinsic value. What our annual reports do supply, though, are the facts that we ourselves use to calculate this value."

- Discounted cash flow (DCF) helps determine the value of an investment based on its future cash flows.
- The present value of expected future cash flows is arrived at by using a discount rate to calculate the discounted cash flow (DCF).
- If the discounted cash flow (DCF) is above the current cost of the investment, the opportunity could result in positive returns.
- Companies typically use the weighted average cost of capital for the discount rate, as it takes into consideration the rate of return expected by shareholders.
- The DCF has limitations; primarily that it relies on estimations on future cash flows, which could prove to be inaccurate.

Analyzing the Components of the Formula

Cash Flow (CF) represents the free cash payments an investor receives in a given period for owning a given security (bonds, shares, etc.)

When building a financial model of a company, the CF is typically what's known as unlevered free cash flow. When valuing a bond, the CF would be interest and or principal payments.

Discount Rate (r) DCF Formula - Discount Rate for business valuation purposes, the discount rate is typically a firm's Weighted Average Cost of Capital (WACC). Investors use WACC because it represents the required rate of return that investors expect from investing in the company.

Period Number (n) DCF Formula – Period Each cash flow is associated with a time period. Common time periods are years, quarters, or months. The time periods may be equal, or they may be different. If they're different, they're expressed as a decimal.

Terminal Value When valuing a business, the forecasted cash flow typically extends about 5 years into the future, at which point a terminal value is used. The reason is that it becomes hard to make a reliable estimate of how a business will perform that far in the future.

There are two common methods of calculating the terminal value:

Exit multiple (where the business is assumed to be sold)
Perpetual growth (where the business is assumed to grow at a reasonable, fixed growth rate forever)

Examples of Uses for the DCF Formula:

- To value an entire business.
- To value a project or investment within a company.
- To value a bond.
- To value shares in a company.
- To value an income-producing property.
- To value the benefit of a cost-saving initiative at a company.
- To value anything that produces (or has an impact on) cash flow.

Margin of safety is a principle of investing in which an investor only purchases securities when their market price is significantly below their intrinsic value. In other words, when the market price of a security is significantly below your estimation of its intrinsic value, the difference is the margin of safety. Because investors may set a margin of safety in accordance with their own risk preferences, buying securities when this difference is present allows an investment to be made with minimal downside risk.

As scholarly as Graham was, his principle was based on simple truths. He knew that a stock priced at $1 today could just as likely be valued at 50 cents or $1.50 in the future. He also recognized that the current valuation of $1 could be off, which means he would be subjecting himself to unnecessary risk. He concluded that if he could buy a stock at a discount to its intrinsic value, he would limit his losses substantially. Although there was no guarantee that the stock's price would increase, the discount provided the margin of safety he needed to ensure that his losses would be minimal.

The valuation method is based on the future performance and the value of future earnings is worth less today than in the future.

Example 1: Discount factor calculation

Periodic yield or cost of capital (r) = 6%.

Number of periods in the total time under review (n) = 1.

Discount factor = $(1 + r)^{-n}$

= 1.06^{-1}

(1/1.06)

= 0.9434.

The greater the time delay, the smaller the Discount Factor.

Example 2: Increasing number of periods delay

Periodic yield or cost of capital = 6%.

The number of periods delay increases to 2.

Discount factor = $(1 + r)^{-n}$

= 1.06^{-2}

= 0.8890.

A firm's Weighted Average Cost of Capital (WACC) represents its blended cost of capital across all sources, including common shares, preferred shares, and debt. The cost of each type of capital is weighted by its percentage of total capital and they are added together.

Formula =

<u>Weighted Average Cost of Capital (WACC)</u>

WACC Formula = [Cost of Equity x % of Equity] + [Cost of Debt x % of Debt x (1 − tax rate)]

The cost of equity is an implied cost or an opportunity cost of capital. It is the rate of return shareholders require, in theory, in order to compensate them for the risk of investing in the stock.

The cost of debt is the effective interest rate a company pays on its debts. It's the cost of debt, such as bonds and loans, among others. The cost of debt often refers to before-tax cost of debt, which is the company's cost of debt before taking taxes into account.

The Weighted Average Cost of Capital serves as the discount rate for calculating the Net Present Value (NPV) of a business. It is also used to evaluate investment opportunities, as it is considered to represent the firm's opportunity cost. Thus, it is used as a hurdle rate by companies.

(1-tax rate) is used to get the post tax value. Whereas 1/(1-tax rate) is used to get the pre tax value. Free cash flow is a measure of how much cash the firm is able to generate after taking into consideration the capital expenses. Thus EBIT* (1-tax rate) represents the post tax revenue.

Example Apple Inc DCF

$$\text{WACC} = E / (E + D) * \text{Cost of Equity} + D / (E + D) * \text{Cost of Debt} * (1 - \text{Tax Rate})$$

$$= 0.9047 \quad * 7.94\% \quad + 0.0953 \quad * 3.2139\% \quad * (1 - 17.14\%)$$

$$= 7.44\%$$

- **Free Cash Flow Growth 5%**
- **Discount Factor 8%**
- **Terminal Growth Rate 3%**
- **Final Terminal Growth 8% - 3% = 5 %**

Apple Inc Discounted Cash Flow

Number Of Years	1	2	3	4	5	6	7	8	9	10
$ Mil.	2020	2021E	2022E	2023	2024E	2025E	2026E	2027E	2028E	2029E
Cash Generated By the Operating activities	69,391									
Less: Capital Expenditure	10,495									
Free Cash Flow	58,896									
Growth Rate	5%	5%	5%	5%	5%	5%	5%	5%	5%	5%
	61,841	64,933	68,179	71,588	75,168	78,926	82,873	87,016	91,367	95,935
Discount Factor 8%	0.9259	0.8573	0.7938	0.7350	0.6806	0.6302	0.5835	0.5403	0.5002	0.4632
Present value of FCF	57260	55669	54123	52620	51158	49737	48355	47012	45706	44437
Cumulative PV of FCF	506,078									
Cash Flow in 10th Year	44,437									
Terminal Growth Rate 3%	3%									
Cash Flow in 11th Year	45770									
Final Terminal Growth 8% - 3%	5%									
Terminal Value	915,395									
Shareholder Value	1,421,472									
Shares	4,569									
Implied Share Price (US$)	**311**									

Margin Of Safety	30%
STOCK PRICE	218

Ratio Analysis

"If a business does well, the stock eventually follows."
-Warren Buffett

57

Ratio Analysis

Investors and analysts employ ratio analysis to evaluate the financial health of companies by scrutinizing past and current financial statements. Comparative data can demonstrate how a company is performing over time and can be used to telegraph likely future performance. This data can also compare a company's financial standing with industry averages while measuring how a company stacks up against others within the same sector.

Example Apple Inc

LIQUIDITY RATIO

CURRENT RATIO

The current ratio is also called the working capital ratio, as working capital is the difference between current assets and current liabilities. This ratio measures the ability of a company to pay its current obligations using current assets. The current ratio is calculated by dividing current assets by current liabilities.

Current Assets/Current Liabilities

Current Assets	162819
Current Liabilities	105718
Ratio	1.54

TURNOVER RATIO

INVENTORY TURNOVER RATIO

The inventory turnover ratio is calculated by dividing the cost of goods sold for a period by the average inventory for that period. Average inventory is used instead of ending inventory because many companies' merchandise fluctuates greatly throughout the year.

Net Sales / Inventory

Net Sales	161782
Inventory	4106
Ratio	39.40

OPERATING PERFORMANCE

ASSET TURNOVER RATIO

The asset turnover ratio measures the efficiency of a company's assets to generate revenue or sales. It compares the dollar amount of sales or revenues to its total assets

Total Sales / Assets

Total Sales	260174
Assets	338516
Ratio	1

PROFITABILITY

GROSS PROFIT MARGIN

Gross profit margin is a metric used to assess a company's financial health and business model by revealing the amount of money left over from sales after deducting the cost of goods sold. The gross profit margin is often expressed as a percentage of sales and may be called the gross margin ratio
Gross Margin Formula = (Sales – Costs of Goods Sold)/Sales = Gross Profit / Sales

Revenues	2,60,174
Cost of goods sold	1,61,782
Gross profit	98,392
Gross Margin	*37.80%*

OPERATING PROFIT MARGIN

In business, operating margin—also known as operating income margin, operating profit margin, EBIT margin and return on sales —is the ratio of operating income to net sales, usually presented in percent. Net profit measures the profitability of ventures after accounting for all costs

Operating Profit = EBIT / Net Sales

Apple Inc Income Statement Sep-28-19	
$ Millions	
Revenues	**2,60,174**
Cost of goods sold	1,61,782
Gross profit	98,392
Gross Margin	*37.80%*
Operating Expenses	
Selling, General & administrative	18,245
Research & development	16,217
EBITA	63,930
EBITA Margin	*24.60%*

NET PROFIT MARGIN

Net profit margin is the percentage of revenue remaining after all operating expenses, interest, taxes and preferred stock dividends (but not common stock dividends) have been deducted from a company's total revenue

Net Income / Sales

Apple Inc Income Statement Sep-28-19	
$ Millions	
Revenues	2,60,174
Cost of goods sold	1,61,782
Gross profit	98,392
Gross Margin	*37.80%*
Operating Expenses	
Selling, General & administrative	18,245
Research & development	16,217
EBITA	63,930
EBITA Margin	*24.60%*
Other income/(expense), net	1,807
Income before provision for income taxes	65,737
EBIT Margin	*25.27%*
Provision for income taxes	10,481
Tax rate	*15.90%*
Net income	55,256
Net margin	*21.24%*

RETURN ON TOTAL ASSETS

The return on assets shows the percentage of how profitable a company's assets are in generating revenue. ROA can be computed as below: This number tells you what the company can do with what it has, i.e. how many dollars of earnings they derive from each dollar of assets they control.

Return on Total Asset Formula = EBIT / Total Assets.

EBIT	65737
Total Assets	338516
Ratio	19%

RETURN ON EQUITY (ROE)

In corporate finance, the return on equity is a measure of the profitability of a business in relation to the equity. Because shareholder's equity can be calculated by taking all assets and subtracting all liabilities,

ROE or Return on Equity Formula = Net Income / Shareholder's Equity

Net Income	55256
Common Share Holder Equity	90488
Ratio	61%

BUSINESS RISK

DEBT TO EQUITY RATIO

The debt-to-equity ratio is a financial ratio indicating the relative proportion of shareholders' equity and debt used to finance a company's assets. Closely related to leveraging, the ratio is also known as risk, gearing or leverage

Leverage Ratio Formula = Total Debt (current + long term) / Shareholder's Equity

Commercial paper	5,980
Current portion of term debt	10,260
Non-current portion of term debt	10,260
Total debt	108,047
Shareholders' equity	90,488
Debt to equity	1.19

Great Investor Strategy

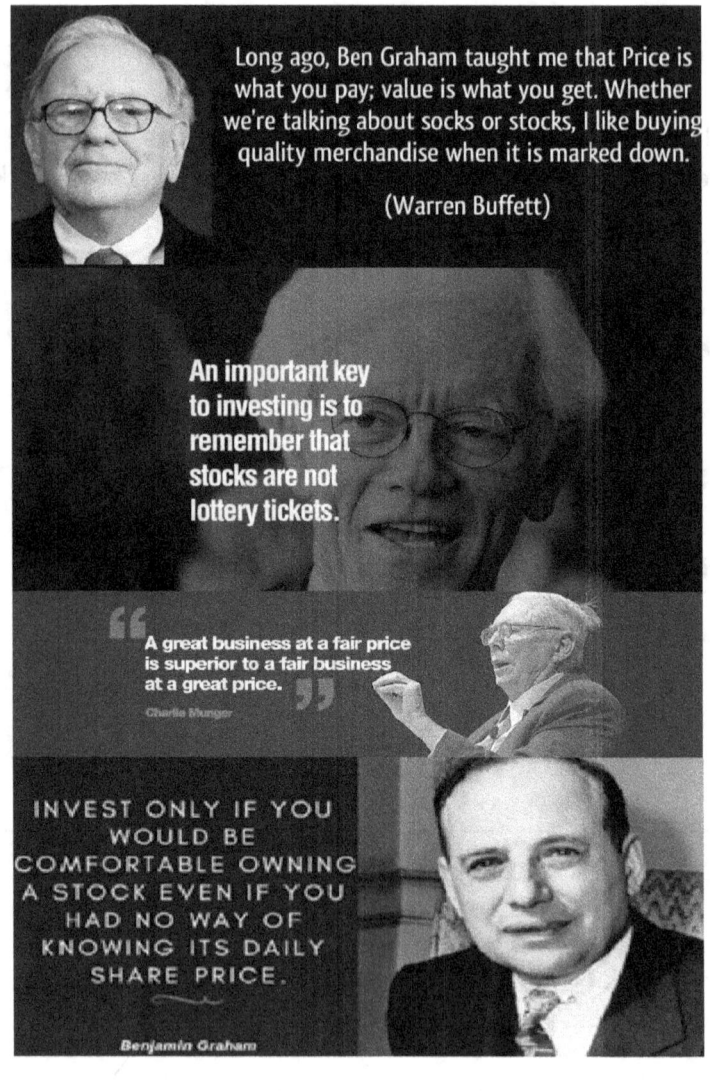

58

Great Investor Strategy

All successful investing is Goal Based and Planning Driven. An investment strategy only has use as a tool to achieve the goals of your financial plan.

"There has developed the general notion that the rate of return which the investor should aim for is more or less proportionate to the degree of risk he is ready to run. Our view is different. The rate of return sought should be dependent, rather, on the amount of intelligent effort the investor is willing and able to bring to bear on his task."

"Chapter 4: General Portfolio Policy, *The Intelligent Investor*

The goal of the enterprising investor is to achieve a higher than average rate of return. Graham laid out four activities where the enterprising investor can go beyond the defensive investor.

We will understand how this successful people become wealthy by using proper understanding market.

The Greatest Investors

- Benjamin Graham
- Warren Buffett
- Peter Lynch
- Charlie Munger

Benjamin Graham

Benjamin Graham May 9, 1894 – September 21, 1976) was a British-born American investor, economist, and professor. He is widely known as the "father of value investing", and wrote two of the founding texts in neoclassical investing: Security Analysis (1934) with David Dodd, and The Intelligent Investor (1949). His investment philosophy stressed investor psychology, minimal debt, buy-and-hold investing, and fundamental analysis, concentrated diversification, buying within the margin of safety, activist investing, and contrarian mindsets.

After graduating from Columbia University at age 20, he started his career on Wall Street, eventually founding the Graham-Newman Partnership. After employing his former student Warren Buffett, he took up teaching positions at his alma mater, and later at UCLA Anderson School of Management at the University of California, Los Angeles.

His work in managerial economics and investing has led to a modern wave of value investing within mutual funds, hedge funds, diversified holding companies, and other investment vehicles. Throughout his career, Graham had many notable disciples who went on to receive substantial success in the world of investment, including Irving Kahn and Buffett, the latter going on to describe him as the second most influential person in his life after his own father; both would name a child after Graham.[citation needed] Another one of Graham's famous students was Sir John Templeton

His first book, Security Analysis with David Dodd, was published in 1934. In Security Analysis, he proposed a clear definition of investment that was distinguished from what he deemed speculation. It read, "An investment operation is one which, upon thorough analysis, promises safety of principal and an adequate return. Operations not meeting these requirements are speculative."

Warren Buffett describes The Intelligent Investor (1949) as "the best book about investing ever written." Graham exhorted the stock market participant to first draw a fundamental distinction between investment and speculation.

The concept of **Mr.Market**

"Mr. Market" and Margin of Safety

Graham stressed the importance of looking at the market in the same way one would regard a business partner who offers to buy you out or sell you his interest in a company. Graham referred to this imaginary person as "Mr. Market," who sometimes proposed prices that made sense, and who at other times proposed prices that were off the mark, given current economic realities.

There are two ways to be an investor:

- **Enterprising:** By continuously researching, selecting and monitoring the "best" available stocks and bonds. This takes time and energy. It is physically and intellectually demanding.

- **Defensive:** By creating a permanent portfolio that runs on autopilot and requires no further time or effort. This requires emotional detachment and a lot of discipline.

Here are 3 key lessons from Graham's book to help you start investing:

- Analyze for the long term, protect yourself from losses, and don't go for crazy profits.

- Never trust Mr. Market, he can be very irrational in the short and medium term.
- Stick to a strict formula by which you make all your investments, and you'll do fine.

As investors, we have the power to accept or reject Mr. Market's offers, on any given day, giving us a leg up over those who feel compelled to be invested at all times, regardless of the current valuation of securities.

Strong Financial condition of the company

- Current assets at least 1.5 times current liabilities
- Total debt to net current assets ratio less than 1.1
- Earnings Stability Graham also loosened the requirement of earnings stability, specifying that earnings be positive for five rather than ten years.
- Positive earnings for at least 10 years, 3% on average over last 10 years.
- Currently pays a dividend.
- Current earnings greater than years ago.
- Stock price less than 120% of net tangible assets.

Margin of Safety

Margin of safety is a principle of investing in which an investor only purchases securities when their market price is significantly below their intrinsic value. In other words, when the market price of a security is significantly below your estimation of its intrinsic value, the difference is the margin of safety. Because investors may set a margin of safety in accordance with their own risk preferences, buying securities when this difference is present allows an investment to be made with minimal downside risk.

Warren Buffett

Warren Edward Buffett born August 30, 1930 is an American business magnate, investor, and philanthropist, who is the chairman and CEO of Berkshire Hathaway. He is considered one of the most successful investors in the world and has a net worth of US$88.9 billion as of December 2019, making him the fourth-wealthiest person in the world.

Buffett was born in Omaha, Nebraska. He developed an interest in business and investing in his youth, eventually entering the Wharton School of the University of Pennsylvania in 1947 before transferring and graduating from the University of Nebraska at the age of 19. He went on to graduate from Columbia

Business School, where he molded his investment philosophy around the concept of value investing that was pioneered by Benjamin Graham. He attended New York Institute of Finance to focus his economics background and soon after began various business partnerships, including one with Graham. He created Buffett Partnership, Ltd in 1956 and his firm eventually acquired a textile manufacturing firm called Berkshire Hathaway, assuming its name to create a diversified holding company. In 1978, Charlie Munger joined Buffett and became vice chairman of the company.

Buffett is a notable philanthropist, having pledged to give away 99 percent of his fortune to philanthropic causes, primarily via the Bill & Melinda Gates Foundation. He founded The Giving Pledge in 2009 with Bill Gates, whereby billionaires pledge to give away at least half of their fortunes

1930: On August 30, Warren Edward Buffett is born to his parents, Howard and Leila Buffett, in Nebraska.

1941: At 11 years old, Warren buys his first stock. He purchases six shares of Cities Service preferred stock—three shares for himself, three for his sister, Doris—at a cost of $38 per share. The company falls to $27, but shortly climbs back to $40. Warren and

Doris sell their stock. Almost immediately, it shoots up to more than $200 per share.

1943: Warren declares to a friend of the family that he will be a millionaire by the time he turns 30, or "he will jump off the tallest building in Omaha."

Only buy something that you'd be perfectly happy to hold if the market shut down for 10 years.

His Advice

- Invest in what you know.
- Learn the basics of value investing.
- Identify cheap stocks.
- Find businesses that will stand the test of time.
- Invest in good management.
- Be aggressive during tough times.
- Keep a long-term mind-set.

Buffett's tenets fall into the following four categories:

1. Business
2. Management
3. Financial measures
4. Value

Stick With Long Term Value Investing Strategies

- Don't let fear and greed change you're investing criteria and values. Avoid being overwhelmed by outside forces that affect your emotions. Never sell into panic.

- Invest in What You Understand
  Buffet only invests in companies he understands and believes have stable or predictable products for the next 10 – 15 years. This is why he has typically avoided technology companies.

- Invest Like You Are Buying the Entire Company
  Treat investing in a stock as though you are buying the entire company. I always take a hard look at enterprise value because this is the total price of a company. In other words, it is the price you would be paying for the company if you could buy the whole company at current prices.

- Companies with Competitive Advantages
  Companies with pricing power, strategic assets, powerful brands, or other competitive advantages have the ability to outperform in good and challenging times. A long term investing strategy requires investing in

companies that can weather both good and bad economic times.

- Find Quality Companies
  Buffet believes in quality investing. He would rather pay a fair price for a great company than a low price for a mediocre company.

- Keep Cash On Hand
  Investment opportunities become available through broad market corrections or individual stocks that become bargains. These are not predictable events; so cash on hand is an important concept in value investing.

- Require a Margin of Safety
  Purchasing stocks with a margin of safety below their intrinsic value reduces risk and provides an allowance for unforeseen negative events.

- Compounding and Patience
  Buffet believes in long term value investing because he understands the power of exponential growth. Companies with sustainable profits can pay and grow their dividends. There are few more powerful long term investing strategies than dividend growth compounding.

Peter Lynch

Peter Lynch (born January 19, 1944 is an American investor, mutual fund manager, and philanthropist. As the manager of the Magellan Fund at Fidelity Investments between 1977 and 1990, Lynch averaged a 29.2% annual return, consistently more than doubling the S&P 500 stock market index and making it the best-performing mutual fund in the world. During his 13 year tenure, assets under management increased from $18 million to $14 billion Peter Lynch was born on January 19, 1944 in Newton, Massachusetts. In 1951, when Lynch was seven, his father was diagnosed with cancer. He died three years later, and Lynch's mother had to work to support the family. Lynch reports that from his early teens he worked as a caddy to help support the family.[8] During Lynch's time as a sophomore at Boston College, he used his savings to buy 100 shares of Flying Tiger Airlines at US$8 per share. The stock would later rise to $80 per share, profits from which helped pay for his education.

In 1965, Lynch graduated from Boston College (BC) where he had studied history, psychology and philosophy. He later earned a Master of Business Administration from the Wharton School of the University of Pennsylvania in 1968.

Lynch has written (with co-author John Rothchild) three texts on investing, including One Up on Wall Street ,Beating the Street and Learn to Earn. The last-named book was written for beginning investors of all ages, mainly teenagers. In essence, One Up served as theory while Beating the Street is application. One Up lays out Lynch's investment technique including chapters devoted to stock classifications, the two-minute drill, famous numbers, and designing a portfolio. Most of Beating the Street consists of an extensive stock by stock discussion of Lynch's 1992 Barron's Magazine selections, essentially providing an illustration of the concepts previously discussed. As such, both books represent study material for investors of any knowledge level or ability.

Peter Lynch may have been the greatest mutual fund manager in history. His astounding 13-year record at the helm of the flagship Fidelity Magellan Fund guaranteed him a permanent spot in the money management hall of fame. Lynch retired in 1990 at age 46. These are his principles for the valuation of stocks.

Criteria for initial consideration

Select from industries and companies with which you are familiar and have an understanding of the factors that will move the stock price. Make sure you can articulate a prospective stock's "story line"-the company's plans for increasing growth and any other series of events that will help the firm-and make sure you understand and balance them against any potential pitfalls. Categorizing the stocks among six major "story" lines is helpful when evaluating prospective stocks. Specific factors depend on the firm's "story," but these factors should be examined:

- Year-by-year earnings: Look for stability and consistency, and an upward trend.

- P/E relative to historical average: The price-earnings ratio should be in the lower range of its historical average.

- P/E relative to industry average: The price-earnings ratio should be below the industry average.

- P/E relative to earnings growth rate: A price-earnings ratio of half the level of historical earnings growth is attractive; relative ratios above 2.0 are unattractive. For dividend-paying stocks, use the price-earnings ratio divided by the sum of the earnings growth rate and dividend yield-ratios below 0.5 are attractive, ratios above 1.0 are poor.

- Debt-equity ratio: The company's balance sheet should be strong, with low levels of debt relative to equity financing, and be particularly wary of high levels of bank debt.

- Net cash per share: The net cash per share relative to share price should be high.

- Dividends and payout ratio: For investors seeking dividend-paying firms, look for a low payout ratio (earnings per share divided by dividends per share) and long records (20 to 30 years) of regularly raising dividends.

- Inventories: Particularly important for cyclicals, inventories that are piling up are a warning flag, particularly if growing faster than sales.

Other favourable characteristics

- The name is boring, the product or service is in a boring area, the company does something disagreeable or depressing, or there are rumors of something bad about the company.

- The company is a spin-off.

- The fast-growing company is in a no-growth industry.

- The company is a niche firm controlling a market segment.

- The company produces a product that people tend to keep buying during good times and bad.

- The company can take advantages of technological advances, but is not a direct producer of technology.

- The is a low percentage of shares held by institutions and there is low analyst coverage.

- Insiders are buying shares.

- The company is buying back shares.

Unfavourable characteristics

- Hot stocks in hot industries.

- Companies (particularly small firms) with big plans that have not yet been proven.

- Profitable companies engaged in diversifying acquisitions.

- Companies in which one customer accounts for 25% to 50% of their sales.

Stock monitoring and when to sell

- Do not diversify simply to diversify, particularly if it means less familiarity with the firms. Invest in whatever number of firms is large enough to still allow you to fully research and understand each firm. Invest in several categories of stock for diversification.

- Review holdings every few months, rechecking the company "story" to see if anything has changed. Sell if the "story" has played out as expected or something in the story fails to unfold as expected or fundamentals deteriorate.

- Price drops usually should be viewed as an opportunity to buy more of a good prospect at cheaper prices.

- Consider "rotation"-selling played-out stocks with stocks with a similar story, but better prospects. Maintain a long-term commitment to the stock market and focus on relative fundamental values.

Important point

- "This is one of the keys to successful investing: focus on the companies, not on the stocks."
- "Invest in what you know."
- "What the stock price does today, tomorrow, or next week is only a distraction."
- "The typical big winner...generally takes three to ten years to play out."
- "The real key to making money in stocks is not to get scared out of them."

- "Time is on your side when you own shares of superior companies."
- "Far more money has been lost by investors preparing for corrections, or trying to anticipate corrections, than has been lost in corrections themselves."
- "In this business, if you're good, you're right six times out of ten. You're never going to be right nine times out of ten."
- "All you need for a lifetime of successful investing is a few big winners, and the pluses from those will overwhelm the minuses from the stocks that don't work out."
- "If you're lucky enough to have been rewarded in life to the degree that I have, there comes a point at which you have to decide whether to become a slave to your net worth by devoting the rest of your life to increasing it or to let what you've accumulated begin to serve you."

Charlie Munger

Charles Thomas Munger (born January 1, 1924) is an American investor, businessman, former real estate attorney, and philanthropist. He is vice chairman of Berkshire Hathaway, the conglomerate controlled by Warren Buffett; Buffett has described Munger as his partner. Munger served as chairman of Wesco Financial Corporation from 1984 through 2011. He is also chairman of the Daily Journal Corporation, based in Los Angeles, California, and a director of Costco Wholesale Corporation.

Munger was born in Omaha, Nebraska. As a teenager he worked at Buffett & Son, a grocery store owned by

Warren Buffett's grandfather. His father, Alfred C. Munger, was a lawyer. His grandfather is Thomas Charles Munger.

He enrolled in the University of Michigan, where he studied mathematics. During his time in college, he joined the fraternity, Sigma Phi Society. In early 1943, a few days after his 19th birthday, he dropped out of college to serve in the U.S. Army Air Corps, where he became Second Lieutenant. After receiving a high score on the Army General Classification Test, he was ordered to study meteorology at Caltech in Pasadena, California,[8] the town he was to make his home.

He moved with his family to California, where he joined the law firm Wright & Garrett (later Musick, Peeler & Garrett). In 1962 he founded and worked as a real estate attorney at Munger, Tolles & Olson LLP. He then gave up the practice of law to concentrate on managing investments and later partnered with Otis Booth in real estate development. He then partnered with Jack Wheeler to form Wheeler, Munger, and Company, an investment firm with a seat on the Pacific Coast Stock Exchange. He wound up Wheeler, Munger, and Co. in 1976, after losses of 32% in 1973 and 31% in 1974.

Discharge your duties faithfully and well. Systematically you get ahead, but not necessarily in fast spurts. Nevertheless, you build discipline by preparing for fast spurts. Slug it out one inch at a time, day by day. At the end of the day – if you live long enough – most people get what they deserve."

Important Points

- "Spend each day trying to be a little wiser than you were when you woke up."
- "Invert, always invert."
- "The No. 1 idea is to view a stock as an ownership of the business and to judge the staying quality of the business in terms of its competitive advantage."
- "All intelligent investing is value investing"
- "A great business at a fair price is superior to a fair business at a great price."
- "We have three baskets for investing: yes, no, and too tough to understand."
- "The idea of excessive diversification is madness."
- "The big money is not in the buying or selling, but in the waiting."

- . "You must force yourself to consider opposing arguments. Especially when they challenge your best-loved ideas."
- "Quickly identify mistakes and take action."
- "Someone will always be getting richer faster than you. This is not a tragedy."
- "Our experience tends to confirm a long-held notion that being prepared, on a few occasions in a lifetime, to act promptly in scale, in doing some simple and logical thing, will often dramatically improve the financial results of that lifetime."
- "People calculate too much and think too little."

www.ingramcontent.com/pod-product-compliance
Lightning Source LLC
Chambersburg PA
CBHW071350210526
45465CB00001B/41